CATS

A Book of Short Stories

Fireside Publications
Lady Lake, Florida

CATS

Illustrations for: Teaching My Cat to Play the Violin
The Cat that was Raised by Coons
The Raising of Phoenix
By Charlene Meeker

Photographs in "Smudge" and "A Chinese Cat in a French Bookstore" submitted by the authors.

Table of Contents

CATS

FOR CAT LOVERS EVERYWHERE

The stories in this book are the winning entries in Fireside Publications' "Short Stories about Cats" contest. We thank all entrants and congratulate the authors of these winning stories. Please read on and enjoy!

Joan West
Editor

CATS

TEACHING MY CAT TO PLAY THE VIOLIN
by Sheila MacAvoy

Have you ever wondered why cats seem so passionately fond of the violin? Why they always look so pleased when violin music is playing? After all, violins were traditionally strung with *cat* gut. One would think the feline community might harbor a fierce resentment to this prince of musical instruments.

Not so. Once, a long time ago, when I questioned my cat, Mister Pip, concerning his fondness for the fiddle, he explained it all.

"Of *course* we cats have an affinity for violins. Think about it. The whole nomenclature of string playing is simply full of cat allusion."

Mister Pip is a large, black tom cat. Although he is articulate and fond of easy banter, I had never heard him so eloquent on any subject as he was of the violin.

"The part of the instrument that controls the sound is called the *tailpiece,*" he continued. "No accident. And, even though the bow is made of horsehair, we do not mind. We are rather fond of equines. It is our insides, our guts, that make the strings. Without the strings there would be no music." He seemed immensely satisfied with his explanation.

"It is the ultimate in recycling. Or perhaps in reincarnation. The Great Mandala, and all that."

Then, after arching his back and stretching his long, elastic body, he turned once and curled into his nap position on the window seat.

1

Our conversation was over for the moment, but a seed was planted. I decided that day it would be wonderful for Mister Pip if *he* could learn to play the violin. This decision became a most time consuming, but a most exhilarating one, both for myself and for the cat.

First, there was the problem of size. Violins, as you know, are mostly made for adult humans. In recent years, beginning in Japan, an inspired movement started, a focused effort to teach small children to play stringed instruments. The method was called Suzuki. A child begins playing at a very early age, as young as two or three. To reach this goal, it is necessary to provide these pupils with very small violins. I felt certain a violin of proper size could likewise be found for Mister Pip.

It did not take me long to locate a violin maker in my town. Of the two listed in the yellow pages, I decided on the party listed as "Master Violin Maker—Quality Violins, Violas, and Cellos; full size, ¾ and ½ sizes." This violin maker's apparent willingness to miniaturize had possibility. I immediately telephoned.

"I would like to enquire about a small violin. In working order, of course," I said.

"How small?"

"Oh, perhaps—," I cursed that I had not previously calculated the proportions of the average human arm as it relates to the violin. With a quick glance at Mister Pip in his still sleeping position, I continued, "—eight inches."

"Eight?"

"Well, maybe ten."

"Ma'am, eight or ten? It really makes a big difference." I certainly did not want my Master Violin Maker to think me indecisive.

"Eight," I said.

"Mm. Well, it can be done. There will be some sacrifice in the voice."

"Why is that?" I asked.

"The chamber is small. Can't produce intensity in the high notes."

"But it will play?"

"Of course it will play," he sniffed. "I don't make violins that don't play."

"How long will it take?"

"Pretty busy these days. Maybe a month."

"That long."

"Lady, glue is glue. We can't rush that part. Everything else can be accelerated, but glue has to dry on its own terms."

I was really not complaining, but my Master Violin Maker had limited patience. I thought it strange. He was in such a patience-needing business. I let that thought pass without comment and ordered an eight inch violin.

"In Birdseye maple or cherry?" asked the Master Violin Maker.

"Which is better?"

"Birdseye."

Naturally, I ordered the Birdseye, thinking it a wonderful coincidence that Mister Pip's violin would be made out of materials for which he had another cosmic identity. Birdseye. How fitting.

I also requested a Moroccan leather carrying case engraved with the letters "Mister P." I did not feel it necessary to explain my engraving request to the Master Violin Maker and he, thankfully, did not enquire.

I had solved the problem of size. Now there was the issue of the musical literature. Any teacher of music will attest that the student must work with music that is captivating and easily accessible to the beginner's particular personality. How vain it is to start a young violinist on nursery rhymes set to music. What ambitious and clever child wishes to be reminded of his or her earlier years? When the violin is placed into the hands of the novice, the imaginative young musician will be thinking Heifitz, not Mother Goose. In the case of Mister Pip, I felt certain that only the finest, most challenging beginning would pique his interest.

I poured through the literature—the early masterworks of Vivaldi and Bach, the practice pieces of Schubert and

CATS

Paganini. The more I pondered, the more I realized that a cat of Mister Pip's size and sensibility was perhaps best suited to the romantic persona of Beethoven. Everything Beethoven, from the very dark and melancholy strains of the Moonlight Sonata, transcribed for violin, of course, to the intricacies of the piano concertos, seemed suited to my big black cat.

I brought home arm loads of musical scores from the public library and copied selected Beethoven compositions onto 5 X 8 index cards. From a tiny picture easel, I constructed a miniature music stand. It was perfect—a silver-gilt baroque item in exquisite taste. Mister Pip would be pleased.

It was at this time that I began to fret, to really worry, about the most serious obstacle in the way of Pip's mastery of the violin. In my dreams I pictured a handsome black cat, perfectly outfitted with a Birdseye maple violin of the correct proportions, reading inspired musical literature that was presented on a delicate and attractive stand, but unable to produce a single note. Why? You guessed it. *Fingering!*

How could even the most cultivated, the most sophisticated of cats, manage the art of fingering the strings? Again, I consulted the yellow pages in search of a competent teacher for a most sensitive and delicate situation. There were shops that offered instruction in voice, guitar, and piano. Several shops offered group lessons, which I knew to be unsuitable for this particular student. And then there was a discreet listing for a local music academy. Perhaps such an establishment would offer consultation or guidance in this matter. I phoned promptly.

"Academy here." The voice had a definite edge.

"Yes. With whom am I speaking?"

"Charlie. Who's this?"

Not an auspicious beginning—although, in the circumstances, not altogether unfair. I considered hanging up, but decided to be assertive.

"Let's just say it's Madame X." I hoped I sounded playful.

4

"Right-y-o, Madam X. Whoa!" Charlie sounded sufficiently checked. "What can I do for you?" he said, a bit more politely.

"I am seeking a violin teacher for a special friend. A small special friend."

"How old?"

"Well, actually, ten or twelve. But—very small for his age."

I began to feel that this was impossible when, suddenly, Charlie offered up the name of the person who turned out to be a truly brilliant teacher.

"I have her business card tacked here on the wall," said Charlie. "I'll read it to you. 'Madam Goretsky, Violin Instructor of Last Resort. No case too difficult.' That do it?"

I repressed my distaste for Mister Charlie's flippant manner and, with trepidation, accepted his recommendation. It turned out to be a poetic inspiration. Days later, after I introduced Mister Pip to Madame Goretsky, I was transported with gratitude to this boorish, but obviously discerning rustic. On that occasion, I shared my dark concerns with Madame, my anxiety about Mister Pip's ability to finger the strings of the instrument. Madame Goretsky smiled.

"There are pupils who never acquire the delicate touch your small friend possesses by his very nature; they never learn to tread a sensitive and quiet course through the world. And," she added, smiling again, "you must admit, with claws like his, the *pizzicato* will be dazzling."

At this juncture, Madame Goretsky turned to Mister Pip and, without the least condescension, addressed him politely.

"A pleasure to meet you, young man. Please, come into my studio and we will begin." Whereupon, Madame Goretsky, who wore softly trailing garments and had excellent posture, swept within the true meaning of the term, into her studio. Mister Pip glanced my way, his lovely yellow eyes slanted into knowing slits. He yawned happily and then, his tail quite erect, just the tip tilted to one side, he stepped forward into the studio.

The rest is musical history. I should not have been surprised that this intelligent creature could accomplish the musical milestones he has. Any cat who can lure an angry mockingbird within inches of his head and then knock the bird to the ground with one paw swipe; any cat who can jump, without benefit of repelling gear, from the roof top to the slender branch of a pear tree over six feet away, without ever missing; any cat who can wait for three hours for a beetle to emerge from beneath a flower pot, can master the art of the violin.

I am happy to report that, after an initial period of training, Mister Pip made extraordinary progress. What tone, what poetry. And, what *pizzicati.*

My elegant small friend is now first violinist in the American Domestic Short Hair Symphonia and has even had a smart tuxedo tailored to his needs. Imagine a jacket of softest gabardine, glossy silk-satin lapels, white pique waistcoat, and grosgrain bow tie. These days, I'm afraid I am so overcome with enthusiasm, my charming friend is wont to chide me for embarrassing him in front of his admirers.

"You must understand, the only reason we cats do not do more things you humans consider difficult is because we have not been asked."

He explained all this to me as he lay next to the pale green Chinese vase he won for his performance of "The Flight of the Bumble Bee."

Ah, the modesty of genius.

WHOOPI'S GRAND ESCAPE
By Lynn Scozzari

"Paging Lynn Scuz-are-ee. Please come to Gate 15. It is regarding your cat," a woman's voice announced over the public address system. Her words echoed off the tiled bathroom walls and filtered into my brain. Listening, trying to comprehend, on the narrow bathroom counter I balanced an overloaded purse, carry-on bag and the brown cardboard box that held my recently deceased mother's ashes

I finished washing my hands and grabbed for the paper towels.

What could be regarding my cat? I wondered.

I expected only bad news since the last few weeks of my life had been nothing but heartache. We were on the last leg of our 2,400-mile journey, making our way home from Florida to California following my mother's sudden death only days before.

We had shipped some of Mom's possessions to our home, disposed of the rest and decided to take her four-year-old cat, Whoopi, home with us. Mom and I had named him when he was just a kitten, not much bigger than the palm of my hand. We thought he was a she. I guess that I thought having Whoopi somehow might be like having a part of my mom still with me.

7

When I heard the voice say, "regarding your cat," I expected the worse. Gathering my armful of bags and the box, I made my way to Gate 15 where an airport employee waited.

"Mrs. Scus-air-ee?" he asked, mispronouncing my name.

"Yes," I answered with trepidation, looking at my husband who had also heard the announcement and had hurried to the gate.

"Come with me. I need to show you something."

I gulped. The winds of my mind whipped: *Whoopie must be dead.*

"Your cat's okay, *now*" the gray-shirted man said, seemingly reading my mind.

"When the guys opened up the baggage door on the plane, what we thought was a black panther jumped out and raced along the tarmac. We wanted you to help catch him, but then our guys threw a large blanket over him. That's a big cat." He smiled. He seemed to be relieved he didn't have to tell us bad news about our giant kitty.

He escorted my husband and me down on a private employee-only elevator to the bowels of the St. Louis Airport, telling us how Whoopi had run among the jumbo jets on asphalt-lined tarmac eluding capture.

Finally, he led us into a glass window-lined room where I spotted Whoopi's blue animal crate sitting on the counter. His deep guttural meows reverberated in an endless loop. This was not a happy cat.

"We don't think he can get out now," the man said.

I put the heavy urn-filled box on the counter to inspect the baggage handlers' handiwork. They had rolled silver duct tape over and around and around the crate—horizontally, vertically, every which way. The men had taken care to leave air holes, yet had secured the latch—one that was apparently no match for a 20-pound feline, scared to death in the belly of an airplane.

Of course, he wanted to escape. His last few weeks had been traumatic. His owner had died. Strange men had come into the house (paramedics) and unfamiliar people (my husband and I) had removed things from his home.

For several days after Mom died, the only way we lured Whoopi from his hiding place in the linen closet was by leaving a dish of fresh fish on the kitchen counter. So when he found himself placed in a plastic animal crate in the bottom of a cold, dark, noisy place, he had apparently had enough.

I can only imagine that he worked on releasing the latch the entire plane ride from Florida and when the baggage workers opened the door to transfer luggage and him to the next plane, he bolted. It didn't matter to him that he was on the tarmac of a major U.S. airport. He saw fresh air and daylight and probably wanted some of each.

"Here's a list of names of the men who saved your cat," the man, who we now realized was a manager, said as he handed me a piece of paper with handwritten names on it. Clearly, they had gone beyond the call of duty. I took the paper and silently vowed to write notes of thanks once I got home.

As we were leaving, the man read the label on the 10-inch cardboard box I'd been carrying and had placed on the counter: "Cremated remains of Jane A. Robison." He shook his head, rolled his eyes and shot me a curious glance.

"Let me take you back upstairs so you can catch your flight," he said. He seemed eager to have the cat-on-the-tarmac episode behind him, as well as the woman carrying cremated remains out of his office.

"You'll be okay, Whoopi. I'll see you in California," I said, hearing his loud meows-that-had-become-howls through the tape-wrapped carrier. *Please let him make it through this flight,* I silently asked the heavens.

"He's a good kitty," my husband chimed.

Because we'd left the gate area, we were required to pass through security again to catch our next flight. Submitting the box containing Mom's remains, my carry-on and purse to security, I again expected the worse—envisioning the navy-blue uniformed security officers sifting Mom's ashes through their hands. Thankfully, after explaining where we had just been and showing the death certificate, my driver's license and boarding pass, a screener let me pass without opening the box.

My mom was my fiercest protector and staunchest supporter. I could tell her anything. She was the only person I knew who always understood me. In a way, with just 20 years separating us, she and I had grown up together. Now she was gone, dying from an unexpected heart attack at just 52-years-old. I may not have her any longer, but I had her cat and he had me.

Over time, as grief's grip lessened, Whoopi became a great source of comfort to me. I'm not sure how many lives he used up that day in November 1992, but he lived a long life—19 years. My vet told me that's 96 in human years.

He became more frail with age and when he refused food and could no longer walk or use the litter box unassisted, the vet facilitated his passing.

While driving away from the vet's office, with tears streaming down my cheeks, I reminisced about Whoopi's life— his grand adventure at the St. Louis Airport, the time he brought a very large live lizard into the house, it's legs flailing and dangling from Whoopi's mouth, and how I had lifted him and taken him to his litter box the night before when he couldn't walk there on his own.

Then, I saw an almost dreamlike vision. In this inner daydream, Whoopi's black, limp and frail cat body lay on the table where he had just died, then an image of a human form rose from the now still feline as if he'd been contained there for a long time. This man had dark hair, long arms and a lanky build. He lifted one leg, then another from the furry cat body as if removing himself from a box. Dressed in a black suit, he didn't look back and didn't look around so his face was never revealed. He just unfolded into an upright position and walked forward, away from Whoopi's body, away from me. He shook his arms and legs, as if to be relieved of earthly confines. And as quickly as the vision came, it left.

During a year of blurred melancholy after my Mom's death, I don't remember if I wrote notes of thanks to the airline workers. I am most grateful they went beyond throwing luggage from airplane to conveyor belt to catch a housecat. For them, perhaps it's a story to tell around the water cooler about the one that didn't get away. For me, living with Whoopi was full of surprises, from his great escape to his final exit.

EYES OF THE CAT
by Muriel McKinlay

The black cat backed into a corner, curved his back into a perfect arch and spit.

"That's no way to treat your new master," Serena chided. She scooped him up from the floor and deposited him on her shoulder, smoothing down the ruffled jet hair with long strokes from neck to tail. "You two are going to have to get along," She laughed. "I love you both."

Serena sank to the couch beside her new husband leaning sideways to kiss his lips. Perseus leaped from her shoulder, his claws raking the top of David's head momentarily as he made a flying exit over the back of the couch into the hallway.

"Damn cat." David jumped to his feet clutching his scalp.

"I'm sorry, David. I'm really sorry—," Serena's voice trailed off. David's face was livid with rage. She tried to put her arms around him but he pushed her away. The ugliness of that undisguised anger and hatred frightened her.

Later that evening when they had reconciled, neither made mention of the incident with the cat.

Serena awoke in the night with the memory of David's face, contorted and ugly with controlled but undisguised fury, imprinted on her brain. Whether her eyes were open or shut, the vision still tormented her. She shuddered. Had she made a terrible mistake sharing her life with this man she knew so little about? Would he ever understand and accept her love for Perseus who had been her only companion in the loneliness of the cold, impersonal city? What if *she* should be the object of his terrifying anger? She wished desperately for sleep to come and end her anxieties, but for a long while she lay awake in the darkness, her body close to David's but not touching his.

From the doorway, Perseus' green eyes glowed with iridescent fire.

It wasn't exactly the kind of vacation Serena would have chosen—a lonely cabin in the mountains of Tennessee, but then, she found herself giving up more and more choices just to avoid David's displeasure. At David's insistence Perseus had been banished to an area in the hallway and only when David was absent did Serena dare to lavish Perseus with the love and attention that had marked their relationship before David had become a factor in their lives. As for Perseus, his distrust and enmity towards David increased and in his unfathomable feline wisdom, he kept out of David's way and David's sight.

The suitcases were packed and Serena had set up the cat pan and water bowls and was just filling the self-feeder when David stepped into the hallway.

"Can't you hurry up?" he asked irritably. "Why don't you just turn him out for the week?"

"He'll be fine here." She tried to sound casual but the fear that David would find a way to dispose of Perseus was a constant leaden weight in her stomach.

"Get your things," David ordered.

When she returned from the bedroom with her cases, the outside door to the hallway stood open.

"Where's Perseus? He didn't get out, did he?"

13

"Oh, he's hiding behind the cabinet," David said, then added sarcastically, "as usual. Let's go." He closed the door behind them and turned the key in the lock.

They rode in silence. Serena's mind was on the open hall door. Was Perseus really hiding behind the cabinet or had David forced him out? Could he possibly survive in an alien city he had seen only from the window of her apartment?

They had left the interstate some hours ago and the two lane road had become mountainous. The drizzle that had accompanied their departure was now a downpour pelting against the windshield. In the light of the dashboard, Serena could see a pulse jumping in David's cheek as he strained to see in the darkness. They were almost past the small café before they saw its lights. David skidded to a stop on the rain-slick road.

"I need some coffee, Serena."

She turned to reach her purse on the floor behind her. Two fiery green eyes gleamed from under the back seat of the van. Perseus! The gasp that sucked her breath back into her lungs was inaudible to David fumbling the keys from the ignition. For a minute she thought of confronting him: *You turned him out, didn't you? You don't care how much I love him. You just want to be rid of him.* But David's stony face kept her silent.

The café was typical of country communities—one room, shelves with canned goods, bread, cookies and a small grill for sausage, ham and egg biscuits, a self-service coffee decanter with foam cups. At the rear of the room, several men lounged around one of the tables. David got coffee for himself and Serena.

"You're in luck," the proprietress told them. "We'd usually be closed by this time of night. We're all listening to the weather on the radio. Where you all headed?"

"Brogan Mountain," David told her.

"I don't know," the woman shook her head. "Them roads may be all washed out."

"Don't you think we'd better turn back?" Serena asked David.

"Forget it. I've been planning this for too long."

Will this nightmare never end? Serena wondered.

The unwanted solitary vacation, the storm, the cat and man game Perseus and David were playing and now washed out roads. And just what was it David had been planning for so long? She thought the vacation had been a spontaneous idea.

Back in the van, Serena looked around furtively for Perseus but he was securely in hiding. The road, which at first had just been scored with water-filled depressions that the van plowed through, soon became like a stream itself and water fountained up over the hood and windows as the van moved along.

Serena found her courage. "This is ridiculous. We've got to turn back, David. Now!"

David's laugh sounded strange and ugly. "There's no turning back, Serena. You're going to make me a rich man. This is even better than I planned."

"What are you talking about?"

"I'm talking about our accident. Those insurance policies we took out when we got married—double indemnity for accidental death. A flood's an even better place for an accident than a mountain."

Serena's lips froze with fear and disbelief. Through the downpour, in the path of the headlights she could see the black iron girders of an antiquated bridge.

Seething waters swirled against the structure slamming logs and debris against the sides.

David stopped the van, opened his door and stepped out into knee-deep water.

"Get out," he said to Serena.

She sat motionless as the water invaded the van. He made his way around it, steadying himself against its sides and opened her door.

"Get out." His voice was raging now.

He reached for her wrists. She turned in her seat desperately trying to grab the headrest to keep from being dragged out. But what she grabbed instead was Perseus. No banshee in Ireland, no tortured soul in hell ever equaled the terrifying sound of their combined, simultaneous scream.

David lost his footing. At that same moment, a log hit the outer corner of the bridge. For a few seconds log, iron rail and David's prone body were united in a powerful thrust of water. Then all disappeared in the whirlpool of water and darkness.

The men from the café found Serena dazed and sobbing on the high ground near the bridge clutching a black cat in her arms.

"We were afraid you'd run into trouble," they told her. "What's happened to your husband?"

"He got out of the van to check and see if the bridge was safe," was all she told them.

Later, dry and safe in the little motel behind the café, Serena looked questioningly into Perseus' unfathomable green eyes. *What coincidence, what mystic knowledge brought you here tonight? Who would believe you saved my life?* For an eternity of seconds, Perseus held her gaze. Then he closed his emerald eyes and stretched.

MEOW, WHAT A DAY !
by Oscar (aka: Dorothy Leyendecker)

"You're going to like this Oscar," Grandma said to me this morning. "We are going on a car ride to PetMart."

Well, not one to turn down a little spin in the van, sitting on Grandma's lap while she scratches my head and rubs my back, I said, "Meow, meow."

Why not, but what in the world is a PetMart? Now I know when she and Grandpa start spelling words like "vet" or "shots," it's time for me to run behind the sofa; but PetMart sounds like something nice for pets. It might be fun.

Grandma got the big soft towel she wraps me in when we go in the car and the pink plastic tablecloth that she puts on her lap first just in case I have an "accident." We got in the car and were on our way. I looked out the window to see where we were going. We passed many cars going the same way and I looked in their windows when we stopped for a red light.

Well now, would you look at that! Right next to us was a red convertible car with Mr. and Mrs. and their little dog, sitting on her lap. The dog had one of those fancy hairdos that French poodles wear, but best of all, it was wearing yellow goggles. Cool! Maybe Grandma will get me some for Christmas and I can wear them when we go for a ride in the van and I can look cool too.

"Meow." Now, look at that black and white cat sitting up front next to the driver of that golf cart, what a show-off. He's acting like he owns the golf cart. But I must admit that sure looks like a lot of fun. Maybe Grandpa will get a golf cart and let me sit up front with him too.

Well finally! I guess we are here at PetMart. The parking lot is full, must be a popular place. But it looks to me like an awful lot of dogs are going in. I'm beginning to have some bad vibes about this PetMart place.

"Now Oscar," Grandma said as she kept patting my head, "you be a good kitty and I will give you a nice treat when we get home."

I think I am always a good kitty, but if it means a nice treat, I will go along with it and I gave Grandma my best purr.

Grandma had me wrapped snuggly and held me rather securely as if she were afraid I was going to jump out of her arms. That should have been a warning of what was to come.

We walked into the PetMart store and it didn't look too bad. Lots of big pictures of cats. I think one of them must have been a cousin of mine or something 'cause it sure looked like what I see in the mirror when I jump on the bathroom sink.

Oh! Oh! What's this? Where did all those dogs come from? And why are they all standing in line with their owners? I don't see any other cats.

"Bark. Bark."

They've spotted me. Grandma is holding me tighter and I don't mind. Maybe if I can pull the towel over my head, they won't see me.

Grandma must have read my mind 'cause she did just that and put me in the basket Grandpa got for us.

There, that's better; at least, those rowdy and uncouth noisy dogs have stopped barking now that they can't see me.

"Next," I heard the woman call. I think she means us, and I took a peak out of the basket to see what it was that we were next for. I couldn't believe my eyes. This PetMart is nothing more than a fancy sneaky way of getting shots. Grandma and Grandpa sure had me fooled. There's the vet and he is holding the needle all the while he is petting me and telling me what a good little kitty I am.

"Mrrow ow," that hurt!

I'm sure glad to get home and I learned one thing that's for sure. The next time I hear Grandma and Grandpa talking about PetMart, it means it's time for me to hide under the bed or behind the sofa.

"Hey, Granmeow. Where's my treat?"

"Oscar, Oscar, you have been so good today, you can have some extra Tuna Treats," said Grandma as she gave me a hug.

"Meow, meow." I thanked her and jumped on her lap to watch my favorite TV show "The Planets Funniest Animals."

THE CURDLE CAT
by Mark H. Newhouse

The Curdle Cat slinks through the moonlit streets. He is silent, black yet almost invisible, like fog. His ember eyes follow every movement of the flickering lights in the houses. He searches hungrily for a soul, a child's soul.

It is Halloween.

The cat recognizes the house. He remembers when he was a pet here, lying stretched in the child's arms, purring as her fingers played through his soft fur. The memory of what he has lost makes his eyes narrow. He raises his ghostly face toward the moon, letting out a chilling wail that pierces the darkness. It is this desolate cry that has given him his name. It is a mournful cry that curdles the blood.

The cat leaps to a limb on a skeletal tree. From this perch he sends his cold breath down on all who pass below. Costumed children gathering candy from neighborhood homes look up, stare into his hollow eyes, and shiver with fear.

They are not his target.

In seconds the children forget and are off again in a mad rush to get more candy before the night is too thick, and their mothers call them inside.

Suddenly the cat picks up the scent of the girl who held him when she was a child. He thinks her name was Lorie. His memory after death is clouded. He is surprised to see how much older she appears to be. Dressed in jeans and black vinyl jacket, she walks with two boys, none of the three in costume. They say they are too old to wear costumes, too old for Halloween—too old to be frightened.

The boys break away from Lorie. They dash behind two trees down the street. A group of younger children walk toward them, chattering happily through their masks.

Lorie hides nearby, knowing what is going to happen. Her heart speeds and her tongue runs across her glossed lips.

The cat feels the adrenaline surging in Lorie's body as if it is his own. His eyes follow to where her eyes are aimed.

The young children, the age Lorie was just a few years ago, when she held the cat so tenderly, when she wanted the cat to sleep on her bed, are just passing under the twin trees.

Lorie's friends rush out screaming, waving their arms and throwing eggs.

Lorie laughs as the terrified prey drop their bags of candy and run to their homes, screams lingering.

Lorie's friends scoop up the bags and return laughing. She pops a toffee into her mouth, almost choking because she is laughing so hard.

The cat has watched it all. He hears the boys bragging, showing off for Lorie. He hears her laughing with them. His hair bristles, but he must wait.

Lorie and her cohorts approach a house on a dimly lit street.

The taller boy, whispers to Lorie. He runs up to the porch, grabs a carved pumpkin and smashes it into juicy pulp in the middle of the road. The boy's rage, as he pounds the pumpkin's smiling face with his shoes, fuels the cat's fury.

The cat's stomach churns as Lorie slides her hand into this vandal's fist.

The shorter boy walks ahead, hiding a grimace as he observes their clutched hands. His tongue runs across his chapped lips which repeat Lorie's name whenever she can't hear.

21

CATS

In the darkness of his bedroom, his eyes reach out to her window each night.

Lorie knows the other boy is watching so she reaches up and kisses the vandal, holding his hand, letting him taste her toffee breath. She pulls away when he tries for more.

"Later," she whispers, smiling slyly as the shorter boy walks quickly, to get even further away.

The cat feels all these things, and wonders how the child he knew could have changed so much. He recognizes the icy cruelty inside her, the anger.

It is almost midnight. The smaller children are safely asleep. The cat hears the contented sounds of house cats as they crawl into bed. It torments him to know Lorie grew tired of him, no longer loves him. He hates her for letting him loose to become what he is now, a forever homeless spirit lusting for revenge.

Lorie's friends are prowling again. This time their target is a car. They swoop along its sleek sides with cans of shaving cream. They think it's only a little fun, a Halloween trick-or-treat.

The car alarm screeches. Lights and windows open.

The boys escape, tossing the spent cans into the gutter as they race down the street, Lorie forgotten for the moment.

The cat tenses, sensing their savagery, but it isn't time yet.

Half a block away, the boys stop running, trying to catch their breath.

Lorie rejoins them, scolds them for leaving her behind. The vandal grins, grabs her hand and they are off again, roaming the streets, convinced they are the kings of Halloween.

A witch's silhouette crosses the moon. It is midnight.

The cat hears the clank of chains and the crunch of locks as the doors of the cemetery begin to open. The real Halloween has begun. He moves toward Lorie.

It is the cat's curse to suffer the sensations Lorie feels, so he knows the girl, staring at the moon, has suddenly felt a fingernail of cold fear rush down her back.

"Did you feel that, Dan?" Lorie asks the tall boy.

"Feel what?" The boy holding her hand sneers.

The cat relishes the fear growing inside the girl. He glares at Dan and Lorie's clasped hands. He exhales into the boy's face, the smell of rotting flesh and decaying blood.

"Don't do that," the boy shouts, throwing down Lorie's hand.

"What?" Lorie asks. "I didn't do anything."

The boy rubs his face with his free hand, the other clutching his stolen bag of candy. "You breathed on me! Get a mint!"

"Forgive me for living!" Lorie stomps away.

"I'm sorry," the boy says too low for her to hear. His eyes search in vain for the menacing creature that he suddenly senses is dangerously near.

The cat hurls his body at the boy's face, his paws cleaving the air and his throat releasing a blood-curdling cry.

The boy screams and drops his candy to the ground.

Lorie turns just fast enough to see the boy running away, the echo of his terrified screams remaining long after he is out of sight.

The cat feels Lorie's fear harden like a knot around her throat. She tries to call the second boy, but no sounds escape.

The cat remembers how, when nobody came to claim him, the poison gas filling his lungs silenced his cries for her in the last seconds of his existence.

The second boy appraises Lorie, suddenly alone. He smells opportunity. He hurries toward her, eyes full of hope. He looks past her, on all sides, to see if his friend is lurking near, ready to spring at him if he makes a move. He wants to take her hand in his own sweaty paw, but knows he must be cautious. As he approaches, he doesn't see the fear that is growing in Lorie's eyes.

Suddenly the boy stops walking. His nose has picked up a strange, pungent scent, the cat's scent, the smell of the dirt of the graveyard, bone and flesh, a musty thickness that envelops his skin like an ever-tightening shroud, clogging his nostrils and burning his eyes. He coughs—a painful fit of coughing— but he doesn't leave. This is his chance at Lorie, now that Dan is gone. He won't be driven away!

He moves toward Lorie again, fighting the acrid smell, stifling the hacking cough.

The cat rubs his petrified fur along the boy's legs. Even the thick armor of jeans does not protect from the harsh scraping of wire hairs against the boy's hairless flesh.

The boy reaches down, raises his pant leg, tries to scratch away the invisible thing that is scraping his flesh like steel wool.

The cat only wants the girl. The boys are insignificant impediments, nameless souls for some other ghost to harvest. But this boy is stubborn. He refuses to leave.

The cat steals forward and punctures the boy's shin with a sharp nail that could penetrate metal. The boy stares down at his uncovered leg, dismayed to see a thin trickle of blood.

"I'm not leaving," he shouts to the unhearing night. "I'm not leaving!"

Because she does not see his attacker, his cries frighten Lorie more than any other sound she has ever heard. She sees only the boy, terrified eyes darting in all directions, hands struggling to hold up his pants legs while fighting off the invisible demons.

The cat strikes again and then again, just deep enough to leave tiny, unstoppable, trails of blood on those pale, hairless legs.

The boy backs away, his eyes now locked on Lorie. A fever is rising in him and he hears his heart pounding. He searches wildly around for his invisible tormentor, flailing his arms to protect his flesh.

The cat, losing patience, lets out a shrill wail.

The sound of all that pent-up loneliness and pain fills the boy with excruciating fear.

The candy bag, long forgotten, lies on the asphalt road, as he scrambles toward the house he hates, but will now hide in every Halloween.

The cat turns his attention at last toward Lorie. The girl is in his eyes.

He makes himself a shadow, allowing her to see his slinking shape.

Lorie is unable to move under the spell of the cat's empty eyes.

The cat is consumed by his need to get even, to pay back those who had abandoned him when he was no longer a cute kitten. His mouth waters, blood red saliva dripping from his lips. He is close to taking the girl's soul.

The ghost soaks in Lorie's terror, knowing she can't escape whatever it is that is hunting her, the invisible Halloween creatures that have frightened the others away. He savors this panic welling up inside her. He wants to taste each moment—to make the torment last until the last second before dawn.

He moves toward Lorie, his eaten away corpse concealed now on this one night by flesh and black fur. On Halloween, the ghost cat is allowed to reshape into the being he was before they led him away with the thick rope into the last room of his life.

He rubs his restored body against her ankles as he did when he was hers.

She looks down, startled. "Where did you come from?"

He circles her ankles again. He has time to play this game of cat and mouse.

Lorie reaches toward him.

He arches away, snarls, his teeth and claws threatening to tear into her. "Now! Do it now!" screams his brain.

She pulls away her hand.

Cat and mouse...He approaches again, concealing his knife-sharp claws.

"Nice cat," she suddenly says, "I won't hurt you."

He stops moving. Her voice is timid, child-like again.

"You're a nice cat," she says in a soothing tone.

He backs away, his fangs hidden by twisted, dirt-colored lips.

"You don't have to be afraid of me," the girl says. "I won't hurt you."

He is surprised to feel her hand drop down on his back with the lightness of a breeze. His breathing stops.

Lorie's hand ruffles his fur as it slowly moves up and down his back.

"Doesn't that feel nice?" she asks. "I'll bet you're afraid too." She lets out a little sigh. "I was really scared," she says, "until you came along."

The cat, feeling the once familiar sensation of her fingers soothing him, slowly taking control of him, stretches out under her hand against his will, his body begging for more.

He wants revenge, to hurt her as he has been hurt, but something inside him is being reawakened by the unexpected gentleness of her touch.

"I once had a kitten," she says. "He was beautiful. I loved him a lot."

The cat tries to pull away. He doesn't want to hear this! It's too late!

"Don't worry." The girl holds him. "I'm not going to hurt you."

The cat can afford to be patient. He lets her continue.

"I called him Pepper, because he was black—like you," the girl says, still rubbing his fur. "It was a long time ago."

I hated that name, the cat thinks, but he really didn't.

"I used to love that kitten, especially when I'd sneak him into my bed," Lorie smiles at the memory. "I'll bet you've never slept in a bed your whole life, you poor thing," she says. "I wish I could take you home with me."

The cat tenses. The liar, he thinks. She is so frightened she'll say anything!

"I still miss my Pepper—," The girl frowns. "I was so angry when my parents told me we couldn't keep him. I hated them!" A tear rolls down the girl's face. It smudges her make-up. It falls on the cat and sizzles like a burning coal. "I still do! I hate them."

The cat peering deep into her soul, knows she is telling the truth. He realizes now Lorie had never wanted to abandon him. In plumbing her soul, he sees she has been abandoned too. He is surprised to feel the hate, knotting inside him for so long, begin to cool. He had wondered how someone could love a pet and then abandon it when it was grown—he had hated her for

26

that! He had hated her for thrusting him into a life of starvation, a life of hiding from predators that lurk in dirty alleys and gutters. He had cursed her for the last days in the animal shelter—for the last agonized breaths of his fading body as it sucked in the gas.

He had come back to lure her to the end of Halloween, to keep her soul with him and the other restless spirits forever, but he now knows the girl is already fatally wounded. She is not the same Lorie that had held him so lovingly in the warm and happy house.

He feels the depth of her pain. He knows that, like he was before her, she has been abandoned, left to survive on her own. Her soul screams of parents too busy to feel Lorie's anguish, to hear her cries.

Halloween is nearly over.

Lorie sits in the gutter, another stray.

Pepper lets Lorie hold him, stroke him. He feels his body slipping away. He trembles, tries to resist, struggles desperately to hold onto life, to hold onto Lorie. He unleashes a final, terrifying, keening wail, knowing Lorie must remain behind, wandering alone in the streets, raising her hollow eyes to the unanswering sky, and letting out a chilling, mournful cry—like a Curdle Cat.

SMUDGE
by Joanne Cameron

I was adamant…there would be no more pets! My heart had been broken for the very last time. The pain of having lost three aging pets in the previous three years was still fresh. I would not allow myself to get wrapped up in another bundle of fur. So, when your first call came, my normally malleable, mommy demeanor hardened. Oh, no! I would *not* let cuteness soften my resolve.

I admit, your story of having discovered an abandoned kitten outside your college dorm was touching, and reminiscent of the first cat I had discovered in my own backyard years ago. The pictures you sent were charming. In fact, how curious that your stray was a green-eyed furred beauty much like mine had been. But I was sure, thank you very much. I did *not* want another cat…not even the "cutest kitten ever." I would not be moved. I wished you luck and hoped you would find a home for your little orphan.

One week later, the voice message you left was urgent. Pets were forbidden in the dorms, and the resident assistant was getting suspicious. Would I be willing to keep the now named, Smudge, for just one week until Christmas break? You assured me your roommate would be permitted to bring the cat home to Alaska at that time.

Of course, I was not totally callous. And would never want you to get into trouble at school. What harm could seven days with a foster feline bring? A *temporary* pet might even be fun. I did wonder how a transport to Fairbanks would be arranged on such short notice, but I chose not to ask.

And so it was agreed. You would bring Smudge home for his short-term stay the following day.

Wanting to be a good host, a quick trip to the pet store was in order. Some kitten chow and two small bowls seemed appropriate, and a few toys would serve as a welcome gift. I could easily pack these items up when he was sent to his *permanent* home.

The following day, I awoke with a smile. I was proud of my new strength in this situation, and felt rather smug at having helped solve the pet adoption situation without caving in to the tug on my heartstrings as had been my norm in the past.

I was a new woman. Hear me roar!

That is, until he walked into the room and crawled into my lap. I was blindsided. I didn't see it coming. In retrospect, I do recall a silver streak across the room, the faint pitter-patter of the tiniest four feet, and the softest pounce. And just that quickly, I knew I was done—my resolve dissolved. Fourteen ounces of fluff had managed to melt and mend my broken heart in less than ten seconds flat.

And the rest, as they say, is history. Smudge never left our house, and four years later, continues to be at my side. In finding this feline, I rediscovered the strength in following my heart once again.

I am a new woman. Hear me purr!

THE CAT AS OBSERVER
by Norman Jolliffe

The dog, Banana, wasn't as dumb as he seemed to be, observed Harriet the little red cat to Baldridge the big gray cat.

One reason for everyone's early assumption that this dog was not smart is because dogs don't start in life seeming smart. Well, cats don't either; but cats get smarter faster than dogs—if they are going to get smart at all. And dogs, if their destiny is intelligence—especially of a gifted sort—start in life giving impressions to everyone of marked dullness.

Banana's case is typical. For example, newly married Judy and Ray discovered Banana at Maggie's Pet & Aquarium Outlet in Bangor, Maine, USA.

Banana's first people, thinking they had made a serious mistake picking him out at Maggie's one month earlier, had exchanged him for a carp fish.

When Judy spotted Banana, she said to Ray, elbowing him, "I think that puppy is unusual."

So Ray turned up his hearing aids.

"What?" he asked.

The other dogs in the wire cages at Maggie's were howling and barking and crashing loudly on the cage wires to attract attention. However, Banana had been sitting quietly and sadly.

In those days, his name wasn't Banana; it was Oddishe. That's what Maggie had down in her registry. Anyway, the jarring and discordant noise of the canines was the sort of sound that had ruined Ray's hearing years back when he played violin with the Bunny Huggers.

His hearing aids couldn't take this cacophony either. They vibrated and jumped around in his ears.

"Honey?" Judy asked, again elbowing Ray. "Don't you think that puppy is unusual?"

"Yes," Ray said. "Odd, isn't he."

"Yes, honey! That's almost his name!"

"What?"

"It's Oddishe!"

Judy kneeled and made kissing sounds at Oddishe. Strangely, the dog smiled back, drawing his lips away from his teeth in an apologetic manner. It was a brief grin, soon erased by another dog, less reserved, who crashed against the cage wires in front of Judy's face.

Ray shouted at Judy, as the hard of hearing are wont to do, "His snout is long and yellow with black streaks. It's like a banana, honey. He's really ugly."

"He's beautiful," Judy shouted back, while squinting— she was very nearsighted—through her thick-lensed glasses. Judy wanted to see if ugly could be splendid.

"Okay, he's gorgeous," Ray said. "But his name isn't Oddishe anymore. It's Banana."

The proprietor, confessing that Banana was a reject, who had been returned late for the money-back guarantee, gave the couple a bargain: Oddishe was for free, plus one dollar, if they also took the cat curled up in the next cage with another smaller cat.

The one dollar was to recover the loss for the carp fish Maggie had given for free to Oddishe's first owners, who were irate because they were late for the money-back guarantee.

"There is no guarantee with this dog this time," Maggie emphasized, referring to Oddishe, now named Banana. "Unless the dog turns out to be vicious," she added, "and likewise, no guarantee for the cat. Her name is Harriet."

"My mother's name is Harriet," Ray said.

"Okay, I made a mistake. Agatha is the name of this little red cat with the short tail. You have to take her."

Agatha hissed, but no one was watching.

Late in April, the day after a bear had broken into their house, ruining two windows and taking food from the table before lumbering back into the woods, the cat Baldridge started observing the dog Banana. The house was already home to Baldridge, a burly and distinguished gray cat.

Early in his life, Baldridge had been considered feral, but had adapted to Judy and Ray's requirement of wearing a collar with a bell attached; but only after being allowed access to books in and around the bookcase.

We are talking about very many books; books in tall piles on the floor; books stuffed in the bookcase, which Baldridge actually read—all of them, those in the bookcase and the ones on the floor.

Yes, he did.

The occasion of the cat's first-time observation of the dog was when Ray was in the living room—as usual with his aids off—working on lyrics for a rock band in Denver called Hard Breathing. Judy was in the knitting room talking on the telephone.

Baldridge was on the dining table in the kitchen licking plates, a thing Judy didn't like him to do. However, Baldridge was rather fond of leftover sauces—this one was an old favorite, Rodvinsmarinad Till Vilt Fogelbrost—and he knew she would never know.

She would know, though if he walked in the plates and afterwards walked on the tablecloth. Also, he had to be careful not to lick the knives and forks, because Judy would hear that (KLINK-KLANK, KLINK-KLANK). Even though she was on the telephone, she would hear. As for Ray, no problem; but as for Banana…the dog, alert to the normal sounds of knives and forks as manipulated by people, was apt with unusual sounds to fetch Judy.

As for the cat Agatha, she was reading in her bed upstairs and, anyway, Agatha had told Baldridge she didn't like sauces.

Somebody needed to wash the dishes, Baldridge thought.

Suddenly, Barldidge heard the slightest jingle-jangle. It was Banana's rattling dog-tags hanging from his collar.

Ting-tang-ting.

Baldridge found where the crusty French bread had been on the table, and lay flat, but on top of the crunchy crumbs. In order not to make the slightest sound, he knew he would even have to breathe carefully. Judy had toasted the bread in the oven. That's why the crunchy crumbs. And she had made a garlic loaf out of it. Garlic! The scent of garlic, which lingered heavily everywhere, might cover the scent of Baldridge, the cat hoped. He crossed his front paws.

Banana entered the kitchen and smelled the garlic.

Crunch!

He jerked his head, looking to his left, looking to his right, but not looking up at the table where Baldridge lay looking down, his cat's eyeballs barely over the edge of the table.

Banana looked back at Ray on the sofa in the living room, then, grinning, moving his lips and his tongue inside his mouth, he opened his mouth and slowly his tongue, like a clever snake, glided down to the cat food in the Kitty-Plenty.

Gently, his tongue lay on top of the cat food. Then again slowly, this agile tongue-snake retracted upwards into Banana's mouth with several bits of cat food sticking to it—almost glued to the agile appendage, it seemed. Holding on for dear life, would be the phrase most fitting, Baldridge thought.

The dog's mouth closed, his lips contorted and there was a very slight crunch, crunch.

The dog's mouth opened again and the process repeated itself half a dozen times. Crunch...crunch...crunch...

Baldridge was impressed. He had viewed a marvelous tongue in action. Perhaps it had a kind of intelligence apart from the dog. After all, the tongue had been bitten time and time again by Banana's teeth. The tongue had evolved, prompted by its harsh environment. It had reshaped itself genetically to survive and live comfortably. (Baldridge had read about Darwin's theory of evolution.)

This is very extraordinary, Baldridge thought.

Anyway the tongue had done its job providing an unauthorized snack for Banana. (Our cat was well aware that Judy and Ray allowed the dog only one meal per day.) So after the snack, wagging his tail, Banana went to the living room to be near Ray.

Ray thought Banana wanted to go out and he opened the door from the kitchen to the porch, and in the process, caught Baldridge on the kitchen dining table.

He tucked the cat under his arm, opened the door again and dropped Baldridge onto the porch.

Thump!

Then Ray returned to his struggle with lyrics.

When Baldridge thumped to the porch, he saw that Banana was down by the apple trees, which were next to the chicken house, which was next to the pile of mixed manures, where woodchucks had their den.

The dog was watching a robin named Harold.

The apple trees—four of them—were regarded by Harold as his territory: the trees, the lawn the trees grew out of and the air above the trees. All Harold's. Other robins, Harold had to chase away. His mate, Ruth, helped in this duty. The two chased away cowbirds and crows, too, because these species threatened the security of his and Ruth's baby robins. Baldwin didn't know how. Actually, Harold and Ruth shared their territory with tree swallows. They weren't a problem. Baldridge didn't know why.

Harold was seriously cruising the lawn under his apple trees, carefully looking and listening for earthworms. Harold was aware that Banana was watching him, but he didn't mind. In fact, Harold was pleased with himself and proud of his efficiency in finding earthworms; so he would show off for Banana while Ruth looked for nest material.

Ruth wanted a new nest.

"Last year's nest isn't good enough," she told him.

"Okay," he said. "Suit yourself. There must be better string in the chicken house. Better feathers, too. Ask Fred for one of his tail-feathers. I'm going earthworming. I'll save some for you."

Anyway, Harold was earthworming. Hop hoppity hop; look and listen. Hop hoppity hop; look and listen.....

While Harold was earthworming and Banana was watching him earthworming, the cat was sneaking, gliding himself with stealth, toward the manure pile, which he reached eventually without being detected by either Banana or Harold or Ruth.

Actually, Baldridge knew Ruth had flown to the chicken house. And, actually, she was talking with the rooster Fred.

Buckbuckbuck, Fred was saying to the robin.

Buckbuckbuck...

Some annoyance on Fred's part, Baldridge realized. Then, from his position on the far-side, down-slope of the manure pile, only his eyes and ears visible to see and hear the action, Baldridge noticed Ruth fluttering from the chicken house with her prize, one of Fred's long tail-features.

Baldridge was puzzled how she got such a beauty from Fred, but he would ask the rooster later. Right now, he was more interested in Banana.

Banana was running up to the house.

At the house, at one end of the porch, neatly coiled there by Ray, lay the garden hose. One end of the hose was attached to a faucet outside the house; the other end wasn't attached to anything. Banana gently clamped this free end of the hose between his teeth. Carefully, he dragged the hose all the way to the lawn where Harold's apple trees grew. The hose uncoiled efficiently (well, in the first place, Ray had coiled it efficiently) without getting a single knot. When others had dragged the hose, to wet down the chickens in July if their beaks were open because they were too hot...when others dragged it, the hose always knotted in several places, Baldridge recalled.

Anyway, Banana was running up to the house, again.

On the porch, where the faucet was, Banana had his teeth firmly fastened to the valve. He turned his head, turning the valve to the left. He reset his teeth. He turned his head again. The hose stiffened with a flow of water.

Quickly, then, the dog returned to the free end of the hose and stepped on the lever of the nozzle. Water squirted. Copiously, water squirted. All over that portion of the lawn under the four apple trees. Harold hopped out of the way. He didn't want to get his feet wet.

Banana watered that portion of the lawn for probably four or five minutes, Baldridge calculated. Then he removed his foot from the lever, ran up to the house again, and turned the valve with his teeth again—to the right—until the hose softened. Then he returned to the free end of the hose and he dragged it back up to the house. He did not try to coil the hose efficiently, because he knew he couldn't.

After she arranged Fred's tail-feather in the new nest, Ruth fluttered down to Harold, who was perched on a tree root an inch above the water.

"What's happening?" Ruth queried her mate.

For a long moment, Harold didn't answer. Then he said, "Can't you see for yourself what's happening? The dog just watered our lawn; that's what."

"Oh, that's fun!"

"Yes."

Baldridge overheard this conversation between the two robins; however, he was wondering why the dog had watered the lawn. The reason soon became clear. He hadn't done it for fun. Banana had done it to be agreeable; to be helpful.

When he returned from the house, having returned the hose, Banana was wagging his tail and smiling. Then he sat and watched the wet lawn. He watched the earthworms come up. Earthworms don't like getting their feet wet.

"Let's eat," Harold said to his mate, which is what they did.

Anyway, Banana felt very content. Baldridge followed him as he walked toward the hard road. Baldridge knew the dog had in mind to visit a recent roadkill to see how ripe it was. Yes, the roadkill was very ripe and with great delight, Banana rolled in it. Then he returned to the house, stepped onto the porch and scratched at the door. He wanted in.

After meditating on what he had seen, Baldridge secured the entrance to the house by way of a large pine tree growing conveniently close to the second floor and a cat-door Ray had installed up there.

As he expected, he found Harriet reading in her bed.

This time, it was Melville's *Moby Dick.*

The little red cat looked up at the big gray one.

"This is complicated," she said. "You will have to explain it to me."

"I will," Baldridge said, "but first, you finish it. Whales are complicated."

Harriet hissed.

"Guess what?" Baldridge said.

"You mean, what else?"

"Yes, what else is new?"

"I suspect you have been observing Banana."

"Yes, I have. And what is true about that dog is what you have suspected might be true."

"So be it," the red cat said.

"Yes, we must accept it," the gray cat said.

WALKING THE CAT
by Elizabeth Kerlikowske

It was thirty years between cat walks; the first one had gone so badly. That cat had easily been persuaded into the harness, but once on the sidewalk, she had wilted into limp nothingness. For a block, I looked like I was dragging my mop. I carried her home, cut the pine knots out of her fur, and she became an indoor cat.

This time would be different. Several things had changed. I had successfully raised three children, so I was a better disciplinarian, not that discipline works on a cat. I was infinitely more patient, and I'd picked up several tips from "The Dog Whisperer" that I though might apply to cats. (I was wrong!) I was ready. (I thought!)

To up the ante, the cat I would be walking was a rescue who'd been kept in a two by three foot cage for two years, and she was deaf.

In the nine months I'd had her, many of her more insecure behaviors had disappeared. She stayed in public when people came over; others could pet her, even men; and she flopped down to sleep almost anywhere. However, she did not sit on laps and never wanted to be held.

CATS

Now that spring had arrived and the patio door was open, she sat at the screen door, her nose alive to the smells sifting through. She had not been outside in at least three years. And she was itching to go. We couldn't let her out alone as a city is no place for a deaf animal.

My husband suggested a harness. I knew harnesses for cats existed from my previous nightmare. He bought the equipment, and we were ready to give cat-walking a try, once again.

First, let me say this cat is smart. She can't hear me call her, which is why she has no name, but if I tap on the floor, she comes. If I leave the room and want her to follow, I pat my leg. She has taught my husband how to play with her. For these reasons, I thought this adventure had a chance.

We put her on the dining room table for our convenience and slipped the first loop over her head. Easy enough. When we tried to snap the other loop behind her front legs, she resisted. First, we only had one leg in; she leapt off the table and looked at us like we were dunces. The second time, we did it correctly as she assisted by relaxing onto her side. I snapped on the leash and away we didn't go.

I slid open the screen door she'd spent hours in front of, and she was immobilized. I nudged her over the threshold, and her paws, used to carpet and linoleum, felt pebbles for the first time in years.

I was afraid outside might be too big for her. When she first came to live with us, released from the cage, she hugged walls and did not want to be in the open. Now, she stayed at the edges of the patio, preferring the euonymus and shrubbery.

Our first walk covered about twenty feet before she wriggled out of the harness in a patch of poison ivy. I swooped her up before she realized she was loose. We tightened the harness.

The second time out, she and I made it halfway around the house, but memories of pavement did not allow her to cross the driveway. She contemplated leaps I knew she could not make. Although her coordination and strength had improved over the months we'd had her free, her deafness affected her

39

balance. If she could have heard the birdsong and squirrel chatter, she would have been straining at the leash.

But her world mostly smelled different. She sniffed out chipmunk holes and stuck her head completely up a downspout where they lived.

Cat walking is not an aerobic activity, but it is perfect for contemplation. I admired her attention to every bug and petal of her environment. There were lessons for me here as we stopped for three minutes to stare at a man across the street unloading flowers. Things smelled that I'd never thought did: iron filigree on the front porch, my grandmother's laundry rack, the light-up deer. All these she learned and they became real under her discerning nose.

On our third walk, she wanted to follow her previous paths as she familiarized herself with her new environment. By this time, I had been places in my yard I had never been before as she tracked the smell of rabbits, and I dealt with welts from raspberry canes. I didn't care that I looked stupid with a cat rope tied to my shorts; my cat was having an adventure.

And that adventure became real when I passed off the rope to my husband for a moment so I could get some coffee.

When she tugged to let him know she was ready to move, he resisted. The moment he did that, she flopped and shrugged off the harness.

I slammed my cup down on the table and pounced on her. It was only logical as I was her favored caregiver, and that might make holding less horrible.

I don't think it was too bad for her, but my arms looked like connect-the-dots, as she turned from a docile empath to a writhing demon in a second. Once safely inside, she sprawled on the floor to invite interaction.

I said a few mean things to her she couldn't hear, but it wasn't her fault. With a deaf cat, there is no tone of voice to hear, no urgency or pitch. There is only movement. The animals teach us how to behave with them; my husband is not yet trained.

Her behavior is more assertive now that she's been "in the world." She comes and meows then runs to the door. She doesn't attack me when we put the harness on. My goal is that we can circumnavigate the property in less than a half hour.

Cat walking is not for everyone. It helps to have an introspective nature and shoes that can take you anywhere. It's also important to have a cat who, on some level, expresses joy and interest in the world. My cat, who watched from inside all winter, is now very interested in the other side of that birdfeeder.

LUCKY
by P. J. Balluck

"I don't get it, Sam," Rosemary says. "You love that cat. Why are you trying to shirk taking him with you on the plane to his new home?"

Sam's fourteen-year-old daughter, Katie, has flown in from Seattle, where she lives with her mother. Katie, Samuel, Joan and their friends Rosemary and Jennifer, are preparing Thanksgiving dinner in their Montana home for a number of guests expected later.

Samuel has been trying to convince Jennifer, their West Coast housemate, that Lucky should fly home to Oakland with her, but Jennifer says she'll be stopping off to spend time with friends in L.A. first. Joan will not be flying directly into Oakland, either.

"You *love* that cat," Rosemary says. "You freakin' credit Lucky in your author's bio."

"He is a freak," says Katie.

"Well, I do," Samuel says. "I do love Lucky."

"So, what's your problem?" Rosemary asks.

"Yeah, Sam," says Joan, "tell her what your problem is."

"You tell her," Samuel says.

"No, I'd like to hear you answer Rose, because so far your words don't make sense to me."

"You understand my words," Samuel says.

"They aren't saying anything," Joan says.

"I dunno," Samuel says. "Carrying a kitty in a cage through the airport, on a plane…"

"What do you mean?" Rosemary asks. "You get to take him in the cabin with you, like carry-on?"

"*More* than one airport," Samuel says, ignoring her. "More than one plane."

"They let you do that?" Rosemary asks again. "As in stashed under the seat in front of you?"

"It's inhumane to dope the kitty and ship him like cargo," Joan says.

"Yeah, I know," says Samuel. "It'd traumatize him."

"It's just cruel," Joan says.

"So what's your problem?" Rosemary asks.

"He'll *meow* the whole time," Samuel says. "I'll be one of those annoying people with a screaming kid, except, you know, I'll look…"

"Like what?" Joan asks.

"*What?*" Rosemary asks.

"Just spit it out, Dad," Katie rolls her eyes.

"Like a wuss," Jennifer says.

"Yeah," Samuel admits. "Kind of…effeminate. *What?* What's so funny?"

"Why do you care how you look?" Joan asks, trying to control her laughter. "And to *who?*"

"To *whom*," Samuel corrects automatically.

Rosemary says, "I've noticed, Sammy, the only shoes you packed for this trip are purple Chuck Taylors."

"Purple Chucks are effeminate?"

"Is carrying a kitty?" Joan asks him.

"Is this because your brother was gay?" Rosemary adds.

"Don't go Freudian on me," Samuel says.

"How's that Freudian?"

"Just put a sign on the cage reading 'Daughter's Cat,' and all the women will fall in love with you," Jennifer suggests with a grin, "and all the men will resent you because you're so manly that carrying a kitty through the airport doesn't even faze you."

"That would be lying," he says.

"Dad, you are such a wuss."

"Why'm I the only man in this house?"

After Thanksgiving dinner, it comes up again, when there are plenty of men in the house—though some are curled up with post-turkey TV and Rosemary's contribution, homemade Jewish-Mormon-Irish crème, in the den, and others are hanging around the kitchen, where dishes are still being dirtied and washed. Because of the houseful and the visiting dogs, Lucky is at the vet's until departure.

In the living room, stringed instruments, rhythm sticks, and maracas have been laid aside, and the women are doing a survey: "Would you," Rosemary asks Hans—asks Eric—asks Clint, "have a problem carrying your cat through the airport, accompanying your cat on a flight?"

"Carry?" Eric asks.

"In a carrier," Joan says. She opens the door to the covered deck, blasting the room for a time with frigid mountain air, to retrieve their dark-grey, soft-sided, mesh-windowed cat carrier, then displays how inconspicuously it suspends beneath her arm from a shoulder strap.

"It's not 'a cage.'" Jennifer tells Samuel.

Hans says, "I'd do it for a woman."

"Does it have to be a cat?" Clint asks.

Theresa volunteers to demonstrate how she can fit her Sheltie inside the carrier. She steps about the living room with Sparkle suspended. The dog's eyes flash with firelight behind black-mesh windows.

"It looks like an overnight bag," Rosemary says.

"Yeah, but there will be all that *meow*ing," Samuel protests.

Eric chimes in, "I don't see what's the problem, man."

"I'll look *effeminate*," Samuel says.

"Dude," Eric says, "it's a *cat*."

Lucky has been an indoor/outdoor mountain kitty since they brought him home in a blanket-lined crate from the Missoula farmer's market one Saturday a few years ago. They at first called him Kitty by default, until he seemed to get into so many scrapes they found themselves saying, "You're lucky to be alive," every time they saw him, which shortened to, "You're lucky, and finally just to, "Lucky." He still has all his extremities and all of his tail, but his ears are fringed, and his plush fur hides a riddle of bald spots—scars that suggest he's withstood buckshot, teeth, claws, antlers, talons. Now he'll be a California cat.

For the first time, Lucky is required to carry identification. Yesterday, Joan and Katie, knowing full well how Samuel was feeling—"Which is not making sense!" Joan kept saying—picked out Lucky's first collar, metal-free, a black-and-white-checkered plastic bowtie to match his tuxedo coloring. When the clerk asked Samuel what to write with a Sharpie on Lucky's temporary, metal-free name tag, he said, "Dinner."

Inside the tiny Missoula airport, Joan sits on a bench to the side of the ticket counters, holding Lucky on her lap, outside his case. He purrs and points his chin up for her nails—"DINNER" big as black-ink-on-white, suspended from his collar. He's been brushed and pampered at the vet's. He hasn't eaten in at least twenty-four hours pre-flight. Samuel has been forbidden from slipping him catnip.

Samuel has checked in but has returned without Lucky's papers.

"Did you even *tell* them you have a kitty?" Joan asks.

"It's not on the ticket," Samuel says. "And I'm not being 'resistant.'"

"Honey, you have to tell them you have a kitty."

"I'm not in 'denial,'" Samuel insists.

"You have to own your kitty, dear."

When Samuel returns with everything in order, he behaves half undone. "If I can't give Lucky his catnip, and I can't smoke Lucky's catnip, can I at least get a belt?"

45

Samuel is on his second vodka rocks. "I know, I know—I'm belligerent at best without a few in me. I've heard. And that's why, my love, I will not go through security until you're out of here. Not until Joan has exited the building."

Joan puts Lucky back inside the carrier, zips it up. He is still purring audibly.

"This Bloody Mary's really hitting me," Joan says. "Maybe I need to sit here a while before I drive home."

"Don't even bother with your sit-a-spell shtik," Samuel says. "I'm not going through security until you're out of here. I can't bear the sight of the tears streaming down your face, watching me go."

"What are you going to do?" Joan asks.

"Nada! Can't I just do this without being judged? I see your back and your lovely bum walking out those doors, and away we go."

"He hasn't meowed once, have you noticed?" she asked.

Samuel pays the bill and they leave the lounge. For the first time, Samuel has possession of the carrier.

"I'm turning my cell off now," Samuel tells her, pulling away from their final farewell smooch. "I'll call you from the other side of security."

"*We*," Joan says.

"We'll call you," Samuel says, the carrier suspended under his arm by the shoulder strap.

"You're all Lucky has," Joan says. "Kitty depends on you."

Samuel and Lucky watch Joan's beautiful bum disappear through the airport's front doors.

Security at Missoula is rigorous, but the line never seems unreasonably long if everyone just flows on through, which eventually Samuel does. After the metal-detecting gate, he puts his change and keys and wallet and cell phone back into his pockets, puts his watch back on, his belt, he tightens the laces of his purple All Stars, straps on his laptop, and asks the security woman for Lucky.

"Your cat, sir?" she says. "You have a cat with you? Where?"

"I gave *you* my cat when I gave you my laptop."

"I didn't receive any cat, sir."

"Just *one* cat!"

"Contained, sir?"

"Why are you wording everything as if to imply you don't know I have a cat? I handed you the bag and said, 'Here's my cat.'"

"Not to me, sir."

"The carrier! It's charcoal grey with black windows."

The security woman walks to the carry-ons piling up at the end of the x-ray tunnel where Samuel first saw her. "This bag?" she asks.

"You *x-rayed* my cat?"

"Sir, your cat is in here?"

"You people have got to pay more attention! Lucky!"

Lucky gives Samuel the same kind of matter-of-fact, proprietary verbal response he gives him at home.

Samuel takes Lucky out of the bag. "Lucky!" Lucky clings to Samuel, not nervously—reassuringly.

"Sir, you need to personally walk your cat through, without the carrier."

"You x-rayed my cat!"

A tall security man butts in. "Sir, please. You'll have to go back through the gate with the cat out of the bag, and the carrier goes through x-ray alone."

"It's been x-rayed!" Samuel says. "So has my cat! 'Cat out of the bag?' Are you joking?"

"Sir," the security man says.

Samuel says, "Are you serious?"

"Leave your computer with me," the security man says.

"Oh," Samuel says, "you *remember* my computer's okay, not the cat who's been x-rayed." He stomps off and cuts back in line. He is now aware of the muttering and cooing over Lucky in his bowtie and holds the cat out before him like Lucky's a baby with a leaky diaper. Samuel watches the security

47

woman feed the carrier back into the x-ray tunnel's mouth and then he steps forward through the gate, Lucky first.

The alarm goes off, and Samuel clutches Lucky to his chest.

Samuel says to the security man, "You *know* it's because I put my stuff back in my pockets."

"Sir," the security man says, "please hold...Dinner...out before me."

"What are you going to do?"

"I'm gong to wand the cat, sir."

The wand detects nothing.

The security man tells Samuel, "Please place the cat in the bag, sir. You'll have to go back through."

Samuel zips Lucky back inside. "I passed through *already* without setting the alarm off, then put my stuff back in my pockets!"

"Sir, please remove any metal objects, empty your pockets, and walk back through the gate."

Samuel takes off his watch and his belt, re-empties his pockets, again cuts in line, and sails through, sans alarm.

"See? What a colossal waste of time! And, now you're going to wand me?"

"Sir..."

"Are you people even trained for this?"

"Sir, please..."

"Are you even licensed to shoot that thing?'

"Sir, please! Take off your...shoes...turn around, stand on the footprints, and face your kitty!"

HITCH
by Ken Bradeen

My husband hugged me and laughed. "And what tavern did you stop in on your way home?"

"Oh, Mark, don't tease me. It really did sound like a cat."

It had happened a couple of hours ago. My plane landed in Atlanta early in the afternoon after a joyful four day visit with out daughter. Melissa had asked me to fly to Houston to take care of our adorable grandbaby, while she put in some uninterrupted hours studying for her upcoming law exam—an invitation I jumped at gladly.

Now, back in Georgia, pulling my suitcase behind me, my carry-on slung over my shoulder, I found the car as I had left it in long-term parking. I stowed the case in the trunk, but kept the overnight bag with cell phone, prescriptions and cosmetics with me in the front seat. I checked the gas gauge and, yes, I had enough gas. I turned the key in the ignition and began the eighty-five mile trip home, still smiling with the memories of a laughing toddler hugging her grandma.

After leaving the airport and luckily making most of the red lights, I entered the expressway and settled down to a steady seventy-five miles an hour. To go any slower, I faced the possibility of being run over by the eighteen-wheelers.

I had gone maybe twenty miles when I heard a funny little noise. It sounded something like a cat crying. My gauges were fine and the car ran as advertised, so I didn't pay a lot of attention to it.

After another ten miles, I heard it again.

A sign for a rest stop loomed at the side of the road and I elected to stop and look around. First I got on my hands and knees and tried to look under the car—a lesson in futility as my vision was strictly limited—but I could see nothing out of the way.

Next, I opened the hood and checked around the engine. I really didn't know what I was looking for, but I saw only a hot, slightly smoking engine. During this inspection, nothing indicated anything mechanically wrong.

I wondered if an animal might be secreted under the vehicle, but no, all clear. Not to waste the opportunity, I did make a Pit stop.

I arrived home about an hour later, pulled into the garage, unloaded the suitcase and went into the house. After the usual greetings, I told Mark about the strange noise I had heard while driving along Rt. 20 from Atlanta and that's when he made fun of me, but he said he would take a look.

"Meow." Faintly, but distinctly. "Meow."

I felt vindicated.

"It's just not possible for an animal to ride under the car for that period of time," Mark said. "not with those hot exhaust pipes and the wind created by driving at high speed."

Mark then did as I had done. He looked in the trunk, although it had been closed all the time, looked under the car and lifted the hood to check the engine compartment. Nothing.

I brought some liver on a paper plate and a saucer of milk from the kitchen and put them under the car as far as I could reach. The next morning, I went out to the garage to look.

"Mark, come quickly. The food is gone," I called.

"Well, I'll be," he said.

"Remember the squirrel trap?" I asked.

The summer before, we had been inundated with squirrels and had bought a trap. It's the kind that closes when the animal enters but doesn't injure it. We had caught several squirrels and had taken them a few miles away and let them out into the woods.

"Good idea," he said. "I'll get it."

I brought more food from the kitchen, placed it in the trap and Mark put the trap under the car.

In the late afternoon, we checked the trap.

"Oh, look Mark. Isn't it cute?"

Behind the bars sat a tiny black kitten. Mark and I both scratched our heads and wondered how this could be possible.

We picked up the trap and the kitten backed away, hissing. I put on a pair of leather gloves before trying to get the poor thing out of the trap. It squirmed wildly, hissing and trying to bite me in its effort to escape.

Meanwhile, Mark went for our Irish Setter Jack's traveling cage and I gently placed the kitten inside. Again, it showed great fear and huddled back in one corner of the cage.

The kitten remained in this mode for a couple of days and I made no attempt to pick it up. I kept water and food in the cage and spent considerable time talking to it. Later that week, keeping my protective gloves on, I reached into the cage and took the still feisty little fellow out.

The kitten seemed to be uncomfortable, but didn't fight me as ferociously as before. I stroked its back and chin and at first it squirmed to get away, but with time it settled down a bit.

At the end of the week, I called our vet and explained the situation. She said she had a cancellation that afternoon. We could bring the kitten to her clinic and she would take a look at it.

"It's amazing that such a small animal survived the trip," she said, echoing our feeling. "It's a male and he weighs one pound and eight ounces," she continued, lifting him from the scales, "and is about eight weeks old."

CATS

Surprisingly, the kitten did not offer any resistance to the doctor when she took a blood sample.

"He appears to be in good shape," she said. "I'll let you know the result of the blood test."

Driving home, he went to sleep in my lap.

At home, we introduced him to Jack, and the kitten reverted to hissing and spitting. His back went up like a Halloween cat. This was going to take some getting used to on both their parts!

What would we name him?

I emailed family and friends. In addition to my father's suggestion of "Lucky," we received about a dozen possibilities; but as a certain amount of politics were involved, I chose the name Mark suggested, "Hitch." It seemed appropriate for a little hitchhiker.

We discussed the subject of his future and Mark said, "No cat in this house!"

He doesn't know it yet, but Hitch is here to stay!

THE CAT THAT WAS RAISED BY COONS
by Amy Gray Light

One summer day, I looked out on the back terrace to see a tiny black-and-white cat sitting forlornly on the wall watching the house. All afternoon, she sat watching my husband Excy, our three cats and me through the glass walls of the master bedroom.

"Look at the 'day of the dead' markings on that little girl's face," I said.

"How do you know it's a 'she'?" Excy asked.

"Just a feeling…" I shrugged.

She had delicate features, despite being emaciated. Besides the distinctive skull outlined in white on her black face, she had white whiskers, 'mittens,' and 'spats' on her front and back legs. She really was a pretty cat, even as rough as she looked.

We'd recently found a home for several strays and, to tell the truth, I had breathed a sigh of relief that the house was peaceful again. I didn't want the additional anxiety of finding another home for a 'lost' and lonely cat, no matter how cute she was; so, hoping she'd move on, I didn't put any food out.

One of our neighbors had 'barn cats' that tend to mosey over every once in awhile to see if they can scare up a better deal. I was growing tired of taking in someone else's responsibilities. When dusk came, I was glad to see that she was gone.

But as we were rushing to church the next morning, Excy called out, "Your cat's back."

Sure enough, there she sat. By the time we returned in the afternoon, she had disappeared again. Then in the late afternoon, she reappeared. This time, I relented and put out a small dish of dry food, which she devoured.

It became her routine to show up in the morning to eat and hang around, disappear in the early afternoon and then come back to take a late afternoon nap on the lawn furniture before wandering off again before sunset.

I sat close by watching as she ate like a wolf. Watching me back, she continuously growled between mouthfuls. Even when she grew used to us and rubbed between our legs, she growled nervously and constantly. It was pitiful, but also somewhat funny.

By the third week, we were able to examine her more closely and saw that she might be nursing. That would explain the voracious appetite and frequent disappearances.

Along with the other pots, a ceramic planter in the shape of a bull, sits on my garden bench. While all the cat drama was going on, a pair of Carolina wrens decided it was a perfect spot for their nest. I tried to dissuade them, plucking out the sticks and other nesting materials and moving the pots around, but they were not to be deterred. Despite the cat's frequent presence on the terrace, all seemed to be well until the fateful afternoon the baby birds finally outgrew their nest and were ready to see the world. Wrens don't immediately fly, but flap and flop around, testing their wings. When I saw the first of the baby wrens hopping and fluttering around the bench, I shouted to Excy for help. He unrolled a length of chicken wire around it, as a sort of "play pen."

This seemed to work, as the cat sat watching the birds' antics, making no move to jump over the wire and nab one. But as she sat quietly watching the birds, one of the babies had the misfortune to flutter over the improvised barrier and land beside the cat.

Before I could react, the cat scooped the little bird up into her mouth and ran across the lawn into the woods. From that day on, with her skull markings and the way she grabbed that bird, we dubbed her "Killer."

A few days later, Exey drove the tractor inside the storage shed and was startled to see two tiny kittens crouched among the farm implements. They peered up at him in horror. Noting that Killer was with them, he quickly shut the door. We brought food and water and a litter box, which was promptly ignored.

But something wasn't right with Killer. By now, she was a friendly little cat, greeting us by sight and eager to thread her way between our legs as we walked or petted her. She didn't want to be held and now she spent her time in the shed hiding from us and crying piteously.

We thought she would be relieved to have her little brood safe from the outside world. We couldn't comfort her because she crouched far away from our reach. While she sulked, I tried to entice the kittens to come to me, but they were skittish and shy, so I stopped trying. I continued to go inside the shed and sit quietly watching until they were relaxed enough to nap or to eat a little in my presence.

After a couple of weeks, they began to play with the strings and feathers I brought down from the house, rough-housing between themselves as I sat watching or reading, wondering if they were male or female and whether or not I'd ever get to touch them, or their mama, again.

Finally the heat of an Arkansas August reared its fiery head, and it became unbearable in the tiny shed. Not only because of the temperature, but also because they refused to use the litter box, preferring the concrete floor. The place reeked.

By now the kittens looked about four or five weeks old. Killer still brooded and kept out of reach. With the help of a neighbor, gifted in rescuing stray cats, we spent one long day and early evening trapping each kitten and taking it up to the house. Turning the utility room into a clinic, we bathed each one, giving its ears a thorough cleaning, clipping its nails and applying flea and worming medicine.

CATS

Both kittens were males and though catching them had been a struggle, both were as good as gold throughout the long process. Although, they trembled in fear through the whole procedure, they made no effort to claw us or run away.

Finally, when they were "fluffed and buffed," it was time to take their pictures to post on web sites in an effort to find homes for them.

After we put the clean kittens in an old dog crate, we went down for Killer. It took about an hour, but she finally relented and came near enough for me to grab her. I think she was wondering where her kittens had gone and did not want to be left behind. As unhappy as she was about it all, she, like her off-spring, made no effort to scratch.

After giving her "the works," we settled them all down into the kennel. By morning, they had overturned all the bowls and the small tray, for even though it was a former dog crate, it was too small for the little family.

We then turned the guest bathroom into a cat suite. The bathroom is the size of a small closet and, since it's also our guest bath, I was mightily relieved when the kittens finally realized the purpose of the litter tray, even though they were not sure it wasn't better suited as a sand box. Then they taught their mama its real use.

When the kitties grew boisterous, I dragged in a two story carpet-upholstered kitty condo in which they could play and sleep. The boys were thrilled. For a few weeks, life was good. They slept, filled out, played and became used to human companionship.

Excy took them to the vet for persistent ear mites and parasites for which they required pills and medicine. They didn't like it, but once again didn't claw or complain and didn't seem at all troubled about being cooped up in a tiny room. At least, it was clean and cool and food arrived promptly!

During the next few weeks, they grew even more relaxed and happy. I could easily hold one of the males, a grey-and-white that I called "Hairy," but his brother was still skittish and although we could catch him, he didn't like it and didn't seek us out as Killer and Hairy did.

By the sixth week, I was desperate to find homes for them. However, no organization would take them and the only lead I got from the five web sites their pictures were on came from someone who wanted to offer *me* another kitten. She was convinced it was Hairy's sibling!

Finally, after browbeating friends into forwarding the kitten's photos and bios to anyone and everyone who might be interested, I had success! First to go was Hairy. Then my parents took Killer, renaming her "Annie," as in "little orphan." Dad had fallen for her adoption photo.

Before she went to her new home, the wonderful cat nonprofit FuRR, agreed to Killer/Annie's spaying at a low rate, and gave her the first round of necessary shots at a rock-bottom price. My parents met with the "shootist" in a parking lot; it all seemed very clandestine !

Mom and Dad endured a *long* and painful process of adoption with the newly named Annie, but that's another story!

Only "Lenny" remained. He was named in honor of Lenny on the *Law and Order* television show and, no, he doesn't keep Kosher. Lenny is a black kitty with a few wispy white markings. Unfortunately, his huge ears make him look distinctively bat-like. "Bless his pea-pickin' heart" was one of the more positive comments he received.

But Lenny had other far more outstanding qualities and, after he got over his shyness, he quickly won me over. His forceful and funny personality and constant chatter charmed me, and I informed Excy we were about to add another into our mix of animals in the house, much to our other three cats' disgust.

To get them used to the idea of a new baby, we put Lenny in the exercise room, where they could all see and smell one another through the glass door. Despite being in the center of the house and being able to watch the comings and goings of everybody—or maybe, because of it—Lenny made an unhappy racket towards bedtime. My solution was to spend the following two nights with him on the Pilates table.

He was so relieved and happy to have company that his anxious purrs made any discomfort worth it.

CATS

After the second night, Lenny was "sprung" and, despite the hissing and posturing, I could tell the adult cats wouldn't try to hurt him.

Finally, after weeks of attendant drama and trying to find good website postings and worrying about finding good homes and the vet bills and help from so many wonderful people—some strangers to us—things were winding down.

More time passed. Annie was still "un"settled at my parents' house and we worried whether or not that problem would straighten itself out. Lenny was a trial for our other cats too, but I couldn't imagine life without out little "Leno," who still hasn't grown into those ears.

Then three short weeks after the cats were finally out of the guest bathroom and it had been cleaned and overhauled for human company again, I glanced towards the terrace one night and caught my breath.

We are used to a nightly parade of wild critters that eat the dog food we leave out for them, but on this night, a tiny black-and-white kitten sat *inside* the largest bowl of dried dog food, eating nonchalantly while four very large raccoons sat or stood in a circle, watching intently.

To my utter amazement, the kitten hopped out, strode over to one of the largest 'coons and rubbed against it like it was "mama." Then he plopped down to groom himself while the 'coons began to eat. When one began to edge too close to the kitten for comfort, the kitten bopped it on the nose with his paws and held his ground. The 'coon backed down and sidled away.

I opened the sliding glass door, which sent all the 'coons scattering, but the kitten stayed put. I stepped back inside and debated with Excy about this new development. My first inclination was not to *do* anything, but Excy pointed out the weather called for rain and, when I looked out and saw the tiny thing still on the terrace, my heart went out to it.

We decided to once again employ the guest bath as a way station for indigent cats. At least by now we had it down pat and were able to quickly organize the necessities for the little guy. (Once again, he just *looked* like a male). I sweet-talked him as Excy crept closer and closer until he swept him up in his arms.

It was providence that we took him in, as it did rain, hard, for three days and nights.

I couldn't get over how much the kitten looked like Killer/Annie and that he seemed to be exactly Lenny's age. Could this be a long-lost sibling? Had Killer/Annie been in the process of moving her kittens into the shed when Excy inadvertently cut her off? She had three extended tits, after all. Was this why she had acted so heartbroken and despondent all those weeks in the shed? We'd assumed it was because she was "trapped" inside; now I wondered if she wasn't mourning the "loss" of one of her kittens. And how *did* a kitten hook up with a bunch of raccoons, anyway?

The little boy was the opposite of his brothers. Whereas they didn't care to be held and only wanted to play, he lived for when he could be held and rocked gently, sitting quietly in my lap for as long as I could hold him. He was totally mellow. He even played quietly. I never heard him meow. If I had the space or resources, I would have adopted him, too. He was such a brave, sweet, good-looking little fellow, and his story—what we knew of it—was so unusual.

This time when the photograph and bio went out to my friends, the same woman who managed to find a home for Hairy found a home for this kitten within the week, due largely to his wonderful story and striking good looks. .

Before he was to meet his "new" mom, however, I knew there was something I needed to do. Lenny and this kitten didn't seem to recognize one another, but if this really *was* Killer/Annie's kitten, she needed to know that he had been found and was safe.

Driving to town the afternoon he was to be picked up and taken to his new home, he was nervous and had an accident. I was washing him in the bathroom sink at my parents' when Dad brought Annie into the room. They looked like matching bookends—just one larger than the other. I held my breath as she sniffed him all over and gave him a quizzical look as if to say, "*There you are!*"

CATS

There was none of the usual posturing of meeting a strange cat, no hissing, no wild eyes, from either of them. They simply rubbed against each other, seemingly at ease.

All too soon, I had to take him to meet his new "mom." When we got to the drop-off location, I held him in my arms as we waited for her car. He sat quietly and with large old-soul eyes, gazed out the window. As I stared at him on my lap, I mused at how marvelous and mysterious our lives can turn, and I felt the familiar ache of saying goodbye to someone I had grown to love.

SAM
by Allen Watkins

At the insistence of my son Anthony and daughter Dorothy, I stopped in front of the house with the sign that read: Free Kittens. My argument that we didn't need another animal in the house fell on deaf ears. I was quite content with the Dachshund we had at home by the name of Zeke. Nonetheless, we knocked at the door and told the woman we wanted to see her kittens. She ushered us to a box with tiny balls of fur tumbling around in it. I must admit, they were cute to see, a mixture of Siamese and—whatever happened to be in the neighborhood at the time.

On my part, the selection was easy. I asked, "Which ones are female?" The woman pointed to three kittens and I chose the one that looked like Mama Siamese. Blue eyes and seal points; my reasoning, have it spayed before it starts falling apart and multiplying.

The kids named it Samantha. "Good name for a Siamese," I told them. The next problem, establish another species in the house where the dog has been king. Zeke took it rather well considering he was a giant compared to the powder-puff on legs; we introduced him, he gave the white eye, walked a few feet away and lay down. His indifference was short lived.

CATS

The kitten in a curious state and now separated from its mama and siblings, approached Zeke with the intention of being friends. There was no malice in Zeke's actions as he proceeded to rough and tumble his new play toy, seeming to enjoy the cries of anguish from the little varmint. Several times we picked up the kitten and scolded Zeke for being too rough. Our admonishments were ignored as he continued to maul his new companion every chance he got.

I warned him, "Someday that kitten will grow up and be almost as big as you. I'd play nice if I were you for fear the cat of tomorrow remembers and decides to pay you back."

The "cat of tomorrow," did remember.

As Samantha grew, we found out that she—that is he—was not female but male. Time for a name change; Sam it is. Sam grew into a beautiful Siamese cat with a personality unequaled by any cat I ever saw. If you fed him something he liked, he vocalized his pleasure all the while he ate. If you were reading a book, he jumped in your lap, lay down and if you did not read aloud, you got a sampling of his claws in your leg. That cat loved to hear you read.

Sam was an indoor/outdoor cat—meaning, when he wanted out, you better let him out. When he wanted in you could hear him knock. It became a ritual, you open the door and Sam looked for Zeke. If Zeke were asleep, Sam crouched, muscles rippling, slipping behind chairs and moving along the walls behind the curtains until he got close enough to pounce on the sleeping Zeke. How poor Zeke kept from having a heart attack is a mystery to me. Having done his deed for the day, Sam walked away to sit in the corner and wash his face. Now who's indifferent he seemed to express.

IN HIS GOOD TIME
by Dr. Janice Wiesen

A giant conclave of cats have sauntered through my garden in past decades. Some assumed squatter's rights and stayed, accepting the available amenities, cushioned weather resistant igloos, meals served on demand, continual supply of fresh water and a sheltering rooftop open to the sky with several overhead skylights.

Should they have desired to reach out to the world, they needed to go no further than step off their patio onto the soft grass for rolling in and chasing chipmunks and squirrels and toying with the newly emerged adult cicadas.

The tall sturdy walnut tree satisfied their climbing and aerobic needs as did the red shed in the corner where their leaping ability was given full reign. The dogwood trees may not have been as sturdy as the old walnut, but their trunks were still marvelous for scratching, attending to their daily pedicures. The cats were fastidious from top to bottom. Seemingly content with themselves, they carried their tails on high, sporting graceful, but haughty wiggles, as they seemed to float on air.

With such a background, let me single out two specific ferals: Phantom and Pirate. They both found me in the spring one year. All of their seasons from then on were spent in their

Amenity Garden with a bevy of transients and residents. Luckily, all was serene, no matter who had left or who had newly arrived. Of course, their first stop was at the vet's office.

It was not unusual to find Phantom and Pirate sleeping back-to-back on my two-seater swing. Neither was it unusual to find them languidly stretched out on my chaise, oblivious to the world. Only their periscoped ears remained constantly on guard.

Phantom was sweetly affable once the mistrust disappeared. I never imposed any desire to hold him before he was ready. I gave him time to adjust. Pirate's demeanor was hostile.

"Don't touch me! Keep away from me!"

Pirate lived up to his name. He was a tough guy, a true pirate with a black patch over one eye; although, his fur was pristine white, soft and meticulously clean, like that of a winter snow ermine. He was small bodied and wiry, the opposite of Phantom whose body was broad and solid.

As the months flew by, Pirate maintained his distance while Phantom came ever closer. I was given permission to brush and comb him. The sight of his brush brought him running to my side. He also wound his tail around my legs begging for a massage. Who received the maximum benefit?

During the passage of time, I noted changes in Pirate. One eye seemed to be closed. He could not locate his food bowl.

When he did find it and took a bite, he lunged backwards in obvious pain and bolted. He began whining and crying.

I tried to get him to the vet, but he was still feisty. I called for help. The Humane Society made three visits with three clever strategies for his capture. These were top priority for his survival; Pirate had to receive medical treatment. On the third visit, feisty Pirate ripped the hands of the helper and fled.

The only solution left was to dart him, but I could no longer stand the harassment of this poor soul. The Humane Society offered another suggestion: let nature take its course. Phantom now kept his distance from Pirate. I have seen this with other cats on three occasions. They can sense illness.

I prayed for God to intervene. I prayed that the next morning when I opened the shades, Pirate would be gone. Other felines have gone away to die. Each day and night, I hung my heart out to pierced arrows, dreading the morning.

Each morning, Pirate exhibited more agonizing signs of illness. His beautiful white fur was gone. All that remained was a naked pink skin, a closed eye and marked evidence of malnutrition. I was distraught. Professionals had given up on him. No one could help me. I had to have him euthanized. It was imperative!

"Please, God, take Pirate! You must!"

Pirate stood his ground. No one was going to touch him. I met an indomitable stone mountain. I had no more fight in me. I was exhausted, feeling his pain and terror. My frustration over the loss of control in my life, in the areas that touched me deeply, was unacceptable. Maybe it just wasn't my call to make. I gave up my vigil with a heavy heart. I slowly stopped beseeching God to take him.

Gradually, something changed. Pirate's appetite revived, although I still had to place his bowl right under his nose. The crying stopped. His white fur began to reappear. Phantom returned to his side. Pirate now used Phantom as a guidepost for getting around. His one eye was still closed and he bumped into the garden furniture. When he found Phantom, he gently rubbed against him. Phantom responded by rubbing noses.

All of that was over six years ago. Today, Phantom and Pirate are still together, hugging the glass sliding door, waiting for their gourmet delights to emerge. Pirate does very well with the bad eye. Both felines sit on the fence looking over their domain and I rejoice in the sight of the two of them, side by side, in Nature's Amenity Garden, their homestead.

Once again spring has returned to the garden. Magnificent color casts a cloak of awe as fragile butterflies abound. Yet, with all the fragility in life, it continues to be renewed.

All the old timers are gone now. Pirate maintains his premise that no one, anywhere, no how, can uproot him. Nothing can change that stance except the Keeper of the Garden of Eden. It is HIS call in HIS good time, not mine. It will continue to always be HIS call. I am grateful that Pirate has the chance to be living out his nine lives in his glorious homestead, in spite of me, and with the added bonus of sharing his time with Phantom, his special friend. Everyone needs a friend. God provided.

ALLEGATIONS
by Karen S. Swensson

It could be said that, except for napping, story telling was his most pleasurable activity. Raising himself up on all fours, Midnight slowly arched his back, rippling each muscle in turn. He sat back on his haunches, gave his whiskers one more polish with a tongue-moistened paw, and surveyed his assembled audience. It was a blue sky, gentle breeze kind of day, and he savored the ripe smell of meadow grasses dancing before him. Mauvaisie purred quietly at his side.

"Hey, Dad!" a bold young voice meowed. "Tell us about the 'memory.' You know. When you lived in the city." Leo never seemed to tire of his father's favorite story.

"Yeah! The 'memory!'" chorused his siblings as they tumbled over and around each other playfully.

"Ahem." Midnight cleared his throat, leaned over to cough up a fur ball, then straightened his back to wait for his progeny to settle in.

"Be quiet, you guys! Dad is *trying* to tell a story!" Leo reached out his left paw to cuff a particularly boisterous brother, who scampered out of his reach.

"Picture this," Midnight began. "It's early afternoon and I'm lying in a nice patch of sun near the window, indulging in my most pleasurable activity..." He yawned and rubbed his nose once with each paw.

"Cat napping!" Leo shrieked excitedly.

"Napping! Napping!" His audience meowed in unison, hopping up and down in anticipation.

"...when I am abruptly awakened by a loud voice. That would be the major's wife speaking in that shrill, high-pitched tone she used when she was upset." He shuddered remembering. "I knew that tone well, having been on the receiving end myself a time or two."

Mauvaisie covered her face with her paws. It had been more than a time or two.

"The major has just left on a trip, leaving me and Mauvasie to keep an eye on her and the kids," Midnight continued as Mauvaisie gazed proudly at her mate. "I hear the major's wife walk him to the front door. She tells him goodbye, stops to pick up the mail on her way back to the apartment, and finds 'the memo.' As I recall, it went something like this—"

Midnight began reciting in his most officious voice:

"15 November 1976
SUBJECT: Pet Control
MAJ Joseph K. Swanson
14-A Roemerstrasse
8900 Heidelberg 1, Germany

1. Reference is made to paragraph 9f, 1st Support Brigade Pamphlet 210-1 "Misconduct and flagrant violation of accepting standards."

2. On 15 November 1976 the undersigned was recipient of five separate allegations made against your pet cat, to wit:"

Midnight paused, scanning his audience. His unruly litter wriggled before him in the meadow, trying to ignore the temptations of butterflies and gophers to give him their undivided attention. He could almost hear the major's wife on the phone, as he related the conversation from memory. He imitated the voice of his human female.

"...I didn't know whom to call," she said. "This is a joke, right? He *can't* be serious. Why would the colonel write a formal memo and put it in our mailbox? He can't just walk down four flights of stairs and knock on our door? Or pick up the phone and call?"

"Daddy, what's a phone?" a voice squeaked from the meadow.

"It's a toy, stupid! For humans." Leo growled at his sibling. "Just shut up and let Dad tell the story!"

Midnight licked each paw and wiped his nose before returning to his "official" sounding voice to continue his recitation:

"a. Mrs. Olsman complained that the cat was
loose within the stairwell at approximately
2400 hours 14 November 1976 and at that time
bolted from the dark to startle her husband
returning from late duty. Further, that the cat
had used the pot containing a very expensive
Jade tree as a litter box."

Midnight always became emotional at this point. "Hey! Who startled whom?"

Mulvaisie nudged him gently with her nose.

"Picture this," Midnight continued. "It's the middle of the night, I'm locked out of my apartment, and I hear a noise. I'm big and I'm black, and it's hard to see me in the dark, okay? As for the litter box allegation, I was *not* the only cat in the stairwell."

"Yes, Dad, but you were the biggest, right?" Leo meowed proudly, giving a small leap for the sheer joy of it.

Midnight puffed out his chest, then continued reciting from memory:

"b. LTC Winston, upon returning at 0200 hours
15 November 1976 was literally attacked by the

CATS

> cat from the dark and the cat further made a
> nuisance of itself in that it would not desist from
> attempting to enter LTC Winston's apartment
> each time he opened the door."

Attacked?" Midnight squared his shoulders and raised his head indignantly. "Okay, I may have been a bit aggressive, but I did not 'attack' LTC Winston. Making a nuisance of myself, indeed! It was cold out in that hallway at night."
Midnight returned to his "official" recitation voice:

> "c. MAJ Little and Mrs. Arcadia had to side
> step a pile of cat manure in the stairwell first
> thing in the morning of 15 November.
>
> d. Mrs. Olsman, upon bringing the incident
> to your attention was rudely brushed off."

"Hello! Why did they think I was trying to get back to my apartment? I *had* a litter box, after all."
Midnight looked at Mauvaisie, who nodded her affirmation. He purred to himself. The major's wife had said that after reading the memo she took a kind of perverse pleasure in Major Little and Mrs. Arcadia having to "side step a pile of cat manure first thing in the morning."

> "3. Therefore be informed that in view of the
> fact that this is not the first time your pet has
> been observed loose in the stairwell all night,
> that effective immediately, your pets will be
> on a leash at all times when outside your
> apartment. Further, pets will not be left out
> all night within boundaries of Building 1236
> to include the yard areas."

"Daddy, what's a leash?" Ryla meowed. She was the runt of the litter.

70

"Be quiet, Ryla! You're 'inneruffing!' Mom, make her be quiet."

"I was just asking a question." Ryla stood up, arched her back, and sauntered over to sit beside her mother, just to annoy Leo.

"Leo, Ryla, let your father finish." Mauvaisie's voice was gentle but firm. She reached down to lick Ryla.

"I'm a cat, okay? Put *me* on a leash? I don't *do* leashes!" Midnight growled, righteous indignation in his voice. "I missed the old days when Mauvaisie and I could lie in the front yard at Fort Leavenworth and intimidate the dogs walking by. *They* were on leashes."

Mauvaisie shivered delightedly. Those had been good days.

"I knew stairwell security would be tighter than ever," Midnight continued, "and we'd be lucky to sneak out once a week."

He returned to his recitation:

"4. You are directed to initiate immediate corrective action to prevent recurrence of these events.

5. Future violation will result in appropriate actions by the undersigned through chain of command channels.
John J. Arcadia
LTC Engineer
Senior Occupant

CF:
LTC Gerald Olsman III
Area Coordinator"

Midnight returned to imitating his human female's voice. "So what does that mean—appropriate actions by the undersigned through chain of command channels? Arcadia is going to tell Joe's boss on him? Joe won't be back for ten days! What am I supposed to do in the meantime?" Midnight paused,

CATS

cocking his head as if listening to the voice on the other end of the line, then continued in his human female voice. "Okay, so I don't need to do anything until Joe gets back, right? The memo was addressed to him. Let him deal with the chain of command. Thanks for listening. Bye."

"Stop fooling around, you guys!" Leo glared at his squirming siblings. Why couldn't they sit still for just a few more minutes? Just wait until he got hold of them all later...

"So how did it end, Dad? Tell how it ended." Ryla circled deliberately around Mauviasie, snuggled closer, and smiled defiantly at her brother.

"Well, Midnight continued, "the major 'sucked up' to the colonel when he got back. That's a human expression. It's kind of like rubbing up against a leg when you want something.

"When the major's wife 'sucked up' to Mrs. Arcadia, I was listening outside the door. She asked Mrs. Arcadia why the colonel hadn't just come down and talked to them. Mrs. Arcadia said she thought he was probably just more comfortable dictating the memo and having her type it.

"For the next year and a half, the dynamic duo—that would be me and your mother—continued to sneak out every time the apartment door opened. The Olsmans, the Winstons, and the Littles found other things to complain about. And when it came time for our humans to leave Germany, they brought us her to the farm..."

Midnight paused, lowering his body to the ground in a long, satisfying stretch. The kittens had scampered off to explore the meadow's wonders.

"I'd had my fill of the military by then anyway." Midnight yawned as he curled up beside Mauvaisie to enjoy his most pleasurable activity.

EPILOGUE: Although Midnight and Mauvaisie have long since departed Germany for that meadow in the sky, the memo still exists, and seems as humorously absurd to the author today as it did thirty-some years ago.

THE RAISING OF PHOENIX
by Amy Gray Light

"She's back!" Excy's voice rang out from back of the terrace where he'd been cleaning the filter to the koi pond. Sure enough, there was the tiny gray-and-white stray cat, skirting the edge of the woods.

Animals are dumped on Wye Mountain all year long, particularly in the spring and fall, and we've grown accustomed to them wandering in from the road looking for a handout. Perhaps like hobos in the Depression era of the 1930s, they've left a secret mark on our house that tells other strays that kind-hearted people live here. If they aren't straggling into the yard, I'm parked on the edge of the road, shaking a bag of dry food and trying to coax anxious animals up to the car. I'm tenacious and the poor things are usually desperate and hungry, so my success rate is around 90 percent. It hurts my heart that they're so scared and yet so utterly dependent on the "kindness of strangers," to quote Tennessee Williams.

We had finally shipped off an orange tabby days before. Judy, our choir director at church, and I had the grand idea we needed a cat in the office as a mascot. So off he went, thus solving the problem of what to do about *him.* Judy named him

Malcolm, after the King who married our church's patron namesake. Ultimately, our experiment failed, but Malcome finally got the home he desired, and today he lives happily with Judy's menagerie in the country. Only when Malcolm was gone, did we realize he had run off the other stray we'd been feeding.

Excy had been feeding each of them on different sides of the house to keep them away from each other because Malcolm had the hint of the bully in him. He was so single-mindedly desperate for a home; he tried to run off any other cats in the area—including our house cats. The other little stray had been hiding in the woods behind the house for weeks and as soon as Malcolm was gone, she reappeared for food.

This stray was extremely feral and wary and would only tolerate us at a distance of several feet.

"I think this cat's pregnant," Exty sighed one day as he watched her wolf down some food.

I paused from washing dishes and peered out the kitchen window. She was so skinny ribs showed.

"Sure hope not," I said, thinking she was far too young and malnourished to have a healthy litter. My mind had been preoccupied with how to trap her to get her to the vet's and the financial logistics of paying yet another stray's vet bill on top of our regular expenses.

The big swatch of land cut out of the backyard for a lap pool that never materialized was deemed perfect for dumping all the tree debris from the ice storm that hit that winter, and Excy had spent hours at a time dragging heavy limbs over and into the gaping hole.

The pit was finally full of brush, limbs, and bramble. Excy waited for a stormy sky and dragged the hose over to the edge of the hole before lighting the brush. After several attempts, the flames caught on, and the pit began to grow smoky as the wood ignited.

Suddenly, there was a great rustle from the bottom of the pit, and the stray pushed out from under layers of jumbled limbs. Scrambling up onto the yard, agitated and shaking with fright, she frantically howled as she ran back and forth from where she had climbed. When she paused and made as if to jump back into the fire, Excy gasped in comprehension.

Throwing the hose onto the now crackling fire, he raced across the yard. Pushing open the back door, he shouted, I think the cat gave birth in the fire pit!" before slamming the door shut and running back to the edge of the hole.

By now, the fire had abated somewhat. When he could see no more flames, only embers, he put on his asbestos firefighter gloves and eased into the hole, careful to balance around the edge. Raking gingerly through the smoking and charred trash, he gently lifted limbs from the center of the pile, the cat now quiet, watched intently. By the time I came out, the stray was pacing, watching Excy work.

As the cat and I stood side-by-side, peering into the bramble, Excy said, "I hear something!"

The next instant, he lifted a tiny kitten up in his thickly gloved hand. It was lying on its back and as I reached out, I saw that its eyes were closed, and the umbilical cord was still attached. It had probably been born just hours before. It made a slight movement with its paws. I took the newborn and bent down towards the stray, who immediately grew calm, and willingly followed me across the yard and up onto the terrace. Excy continued to rake through the brush but found no other babies.

The black kitten fit into the palm of my hand, and except for a tiny spot on one pad of her front paw, she was unharmed. I slipped inside and was soon back with some salve and a box. The stray actually sat still as I ran my hands over her body, examining her for injuries. I could see only one teat extended, another sign that this was her only kitten. I watched as she rearranged the worn towel in the box, making a nest for her baby. Later that afternoon, we moved the little family into Excy's studio.

That night there was a horrific thunderstorm. The next morning the pit overflowed with cold and dingy gray rainwater.

It's been four years since that fateful summer day, and while M.C. (Mama Cat) still lives aloofly in the studio, Phoenix, who is sleek and shiny as a seal despite allowing no brushing, shares our house with us and our other two cats, racing down hallways, playing hide-and-seek, sloshing her paws in the water dishes (she only believes in drinking moving water), and chattering about the latest moth that fluttered its way inside the house.

When Excy leaves the house each night to give the horses their late-night snack, she waits anxiously at the window for him to return. He cannot repair to the bathroom alone, and the entire time they are together, she talks incessantly.

I can't pretend it hasn't made me jealous, for aside from playing laser tag, from the beginning, she barely registered my presence; as a "cat person" of long standing, it had begun to drive me batty. So I waged a campaign to woo her, which entailed bribing her with certain cat treats she has quickly become addicted to.

After establishing myself as the sole dispenser of the treats, she has gone from flinching when I stroke her to following me around and sleeping near me on the bed. But for most pats and kisses on the nose, treats are expected, and she still doesn't care for strokes.

As she jumps up by her dish and licks her lips in anticipation, I have to wonder, who's bribing whom? Regardless, as she was raised from the ashes, so too has Phoenix lit up our world.

CHESSIE CAT
by Jennifer Ballard

By the time I got to work, almost all the dogs with grooming appointments had arrived. I had clipped, bathed and brushed out a poodle before Lisa brought in my last client for the day, a Doberman that she put in the big cage out in the hall.

"Is this the last one you're expecting, Teri?" she asked me, over the sound of the clippers I was using to trim a schnauzer.

"I think so. I have a short day; just the two Hensley's Scotties, the Yorkie, the doberman that's only getting a bath and this one."

"Who's the cat?" she asked.

I looked up from my clipping. "What cat?"

"The one in the cage above the doberman."

I turned off the clippers and followed Lisa out into the hall. We looked at the enormous, long haired, white cat.

It wasn't just a fluffy white cat. It looked like a cross between a Maine Coon and a Persian. It had the longest, thickest, most beautiful coat I'd ever seen. It wasn't solid white, but had light patches of grey and orange, so faint they looked like smudges on the surface of the fur.

"Is it in the book?" she asked.

77

I checked my appointment book, counted the dogs and marked them off.

"No."

My grooming shop was one room rented in the back of a small veterinary clinic. The only staff were Dr. Steve, the vet, and Lisa, who acted as both vet tech and receptionist.

Lisa often accepted appointments for me. If I didn't have a lot scheduled, she would add them without notifying me. I sometimes got calls for appointments on my cell or at home and occasionally forgot to write them in the book.

"I don't remember any calls for it," I said. "Could it be a patient?"

"I don't think so," Lisa said. "Steve's not in yet; he can't have brought it. It wasn't here when I brought the dogs back."

She checked Steve's appointments, but there was nothing about a cat.

"Is it a regular?" Lisa asked. "Do you recognize it?"

I did have a few cats I groomed regularly, but this wasn't one of them. Neither of us recognized it, and we would have.

It was possible someone had brought it in while I was bathing the poodle, but it was hard to imagine anyone being in the building without Lisa or me knowing about it, as small as the clinic was. There were only two short hallways, and you had to walk through each room to get to another.

The back door was in the kennel room where the bathtub was. There was a side door, but it was kept locked until Steve came in. Lisa checked it; it was still locked.

All the animals were accounted for, except the cat.

"Think you should groom it?" she asked.

We looked at the cat again. Most cats did not like grooming, especially being bathed, and there were some Steve had to tranquilize for me to work on. This cat's coat was in pretty good shape; it clearly got brushed at least occasionally.

I pulled the cat out of the cage. Holding it, carefully balancing its massive weight, and ran my hands through its fur. The cat rested comfortably in my arms, purring lightly.

"Her coat is getting a little matted," I said. "I don't see any fleas, but her skin has some rough patches and looks sensitive. I'll try to bathe her and see how she is. It can't hurt."

I removed the worst of the small mats from her fur before taking her to the tub for a bath. She was quiet and cooperative, although clearly not a fan of the process. She wasn't fond of having the dryer blowing on her either, but held still for me to brush her coat out. When I finished, she purred loudly as I carried her back to her cage.

I cleaned up and was ready to leave by noon.

On my way out, I noticed the cat was gone. I stopped up front where Steve and Lisa were enjoying the short break they took at lunchtime.

"Someone picked up the cat," I said. "Whose was it?"

"Is it gone?" Lisa asked.

"It didn't pass through here," Steve said.

It would be hard for a cat that big to come or go without someone seeing it. We couldn't imagine that it had snuck out one of the doors when someone came or went. It would have been noticed.

The three of us searched the entire building and didn't find the cat.

"It can't still be here," Steve said. "It's too big to hide anywhere."

I walked around the yard and checked with the homeowners and business owners of the few nearby buildings. No one had seen the cat.

"Well, unless someone turns up looking for it, I guess we don't need to worry about it," Steve said.

While I worried anyway and suspected they did too, there wasn't anything to do about it, so I went home.

"Did anyone come in yesterday afternoon, looking for a big white cat?" I asked as soon as I arrived the next day.

"Nope," Steve said. "Lisa asked all the grooming clients when they came in to pick up their dogs if they had brought a cat in for grooming."

"Maybe I shouldn't have," she added. "Some of them looked a little worried that we had an animal unaccounted for.

79

She handed me my appointment book, with the checks tucked carefully inside.

"There are checks for all the dogs yesterday and fifty dollars in cash," I said. "Who did the cash come from?"

"I didn't take any cash," Lisa said.

"Maybe it was for the cat," Steve suggested.

"No one picked up the cat."

"And no one left the money," he said. "The money appeared; the cat disappeared. Makes perfect sense.

Three weeks later, the mystery client showed up again in the same cage. And again three weeks after that. I nicknamed her Chessie Cat, after the disappearing and reappearing feline in the Lewis Carroll book. No one saw her come in or go out and again there was cash with the checks in the desk drawer that no one claimed to have put there.

One day just after we'd had a visit from Chessie, I came in to find Lisa trying to politely deal with a difficult customer—or non-customer, as it turned out.

"I'm just trying to do the right thing," the man said. "I'm not the person that hit it. I couldn't just leave it in the road, but I'm not paying for any vet costs. It's not my cat and I don't want it."

"I understand, sir," Lisa said. "Thank you, we'll take care of it."

She smiled, though I knew she was annoyed at the man's attitude. Slightly surprised by her polite acceptance, he nodded stiffly and made a quick escape, almost bumping into me on his way out.

We were faced with this situation on occasion, mostly with animal lovers who were truly distressed at leaving an animal, claiming it wasn't theirs and they couldn't afford any responsibility for its care. Sometimes the cat or dog brought in was hurt or sick, but not always. People brought them to us rather than the shelter as if we had a better chance of finding homes for them.

I looked at the kitten Lisa held, a brown and tan Siamese-type with blue eyes. It looked more traumatized than hurt but Steve would have to look at it before we could be sure.

"I guess we're lucky he didn't drive on and leave it in the street," I said.

"He's gorgeous," she said. "Which one of us will end up with it, if we don't find it a home?"

"None of us needs any more animals," I said.

That was true, but when a cat or dog came in that we couldn't adopt out, it seemed like one of us always took it home.

Steve kept his two hunting dogs in the yard at the clinic because he lived in an apartment where no pets are allowed.

Lisa and I each had small houses with small yards, and each of us had three dogs and three cats.

A week later, I put the kitten in my car to take home with me—just until I could find it a permanent home. It had squealed and squalled when I put it in a travel cage, so I decided letting it ride loose in the car might be less distracting. While I drove, the kitten curled up on the seat and purred quietly.

My route home had been blocked by road construction for weeks, and the detour was a complicated path over badly kept back roads. With half my attention on the kitten, whose nap was disturbed by the rough ride, I missed avoiding a pothole and one of my back tires blew.

The kitten wasn't nearly as alarmed as I was when the car skidded across the rough pavement and slid to a stop in front of a small house. As I changed the tire, he watched me through the car window, attracting the attention of a small girl from the house.

"Cute kitten," she said.

"You want it?" I asked, trying not to sound irritable.

I didn't like to admit it, but it wasn't just the ruined tire that bothered me. I really didn't want to keep another cat, and knew I could easily get attached to this one.

"Can't," the girl said. "Sister's allergic."

"Know anyone who might want it?"

"Lady down the street might. Ms. Baker."

"Do you know which house?"

"Gray house at the end of the street. Big house, big yard, lots of trees."

I knew the one she meant. Every day I had driven this road for the past few weeks, I always admired the collection of cats and dogs that adorned the yard and huge front porch.

I drove slowly up the road and found the old gray house. It was ancient but neatly kept and today two cats and three dogs were scattered across the porch. All of them looked well cared for and healthy.

I debated with myself about carrying the kitten up to the door. He didn't get ruffled easily, so I decided to risk it. The cats and dogs didn't react to us other than to watch me with polite interest and wag their tails. They weren't upset by the kitten and he wasn't nervous about being surrounded by strange animals.

My light knock on the door was answered by a small woman who, at first glance, looked as old as the house. The age implied by the wrinkles on her face was countered by the youth in her eyes, voice and graceful movements.

"Mrs. Baker?" I asked.

"Yes, I am AnnaLee Baker," she said.

"I'm Teri Locke. I work at a vet clinic and we're looking for a home for this abandoned kitten," I said. "One of your neighbors said you might want him. He's been neutered and wormed and had all his shots."

"He's lovely," AnnaLee said.

She reached for the kitten and I gently handed it to her. She held it for a few minutes, the kitten purring louder by the second.

"I believe I can keep another cat," she said.

The other animals circled at our feet. They sniffed at the kitten and accepted it without fuss. I had no doubt the kitten would be happy here.

Two dogs followed us as AnnaLee walked to my car with me.

"Your animals are very content," I said, petting a friendly, tall and shaggy something.

"That's Brutus," she said.

She told me Brutus' littermate was Bruno, the slightly shorter, sleek hound that also pranced beside us. Speedy was the Bassett Hound who hadn't gotten up to follow us into the yard.

I looked back at the collection of pets on the porch and saw a familiar cat among them. I didn't remember seeing him while driving by before, but Chessie was unmistakable from such a short distance.

"Mrs. Baker," I said, "that cat is…"

I stopped and looked around. The little woman had disappeared.

LITTLE UGLY
by Joye O'Keefe

"FREE KITTENS," the sign said.

"Oh!" exclaimed Mark. "Let's stop and see the kittens. Can we have one, Mom?"

"Yeah Mom, *Please*?" Beth echoed.

"We'll stop and look, but I'm not sure we're ready for another cat right now," their Mom said. She was thinking of Sammy, their beloved cat who had died of old age just last week. They still missed him.

There were six playful kittens. Two were calico with beautiful markings. Two were black and white, with mask-like markings across their eyes. One had beautiful, soft, long, gray fur; however, the last kitten hardly received a glance from the children.

His fur was medium length and silky, but he was black with splotches of gray and tan, all mixed together. It looked like he'd been splattered with all the colors and then a hand had smeared them into an unattractive mess. There was no white to lighten his dark, dismal coloring.

The kids fell in love with the gray one. Even Mom couldn't resist, so "Smokey" became the first kitten to find a home.

As the days passed, one by one, the kittens found homes—all except "Little Ugly." When folks stopped to see the kittens, he'd run to them, rub against their legs and purr loudly to get their attention, but no one wanted him. He was very lonely when all his brothers and sister had left.

Several people stopped to see him, but no one wanted to take him home. He became more and more lonely.

One day a car pulled in, but the kitten knew it wouldn't be anyone for him to love. He continued to lie in the sun and pretended to be asleep.

"Just one left," said the owner. "Not much to look at, but a nice cat nevertheless."

Little Ugly felt himself being lifted into the arms of a little girl. "Oh, how sweet! What a lovely, soft kitten," she crooned, as she petted him gently and held him close.

Little Ugly couldn't believe his ears! She didn't seem to find him ugly. He started to purr and snuggled in her arms.

"Can I keep him, Daddy? Please! He's just perfect."

"Of course, Anne," her dad answered. "That's why we came, to find a kitten to keep you company."

"Thank you, Daddy. I'm going to call him "Handsome Hairy" and just Handsome for short. I'll take very good care of him, I promise." She smiled and her blue eyes sparkled.

Anne walked slowly back towards the car while Handsome Hairy's former owner shook his head, perplexed.

"You're certainly welcome to the kitten, but he's just not a beautiful cat—never will be."

Anne's dad said, "That's because you only see the outside. Anne sees the heart and goodness within. You see, he smiled gently, "my daughter's blind."

LEROY, THE TALKING CAT
by Taylor Shaye

LeRoy! What a dumb name for a cat. Somehow it stuck, and he never objected. When someone called him, he just sat there like the king of the house with a shitty grin on his face. Most times, if I happened to be nearby, he meandered over, rubbed his warm fur against my leg and looked up at me with those big grey eyes until I rudely shooed him away.

"Sue," I'd yell. "didn't I tell you to get rid of this damn cat? You know I don't like animals in the house."

My youngest daughter, all of twelve-years-old, would then pick him up and cuddle him, once again making profound promises to find him a good home. Promises, which we both knew she wouldn't keep.

I'm not a bad person you understand. I just don't like animals—especially cats—especially cats named Leroy. Couldn't those kids find a more creative name to call him? Sue shouldn't have brought him home in the first place, but she never could resist a stray without a home.

I don't remember just how long LeRoy lived with us. The months stretched into years and I developed a degree of tolerance, I still didn't like him, but I found I could tolerate him. No matter how much Leroy was ignored, he wouldn't leave. He kept doing his best to make friends with me.

I gradually started developing some respect for him, even laughing at some of his antics. The times I looked out the door and saw him near the top of a telephone pole starting to walk across the wires to capture a bird resting quietly in front of him then teetering precariously when he reached a paw toward the bird and it wisely flew away, I held my breath, afraid he would fall. But he never did. He quietly moved on to greener pastures—my backyard.

Those were the years we lived in a large three-story house near the center of a small town. The house, sitting on nearly an acre of treed land near the downtown area, had once been a showplace with its tall stately maples and oak trees scattered around the back yard, a weeping willow shielding the sunny side of the detached garage and a lone snowball tree in the front side yard. Its circular gravel driveway made a perfect arc from the busy street to the garage then wound its way through the trees to cut a path between our home and the house next door with barely enough room for a car to maneuver over the bricked section finding its way back to the street.

The backyard was Leroy's favorite spot where a plethora of small animals and birds gathered to thrill visitors. Well, visitors other than my brother who parked his car next to the garage for a few days. He came to retrieve it and was attacked by a half dozen blue jays as he rushed to get inside the car. Leroy sat quietly by and smirked.

Spring yielded to summer and we all spent more time outside. I noticed LeRoy trying harder to get my approval, purring joyfully when I hesitantly patted him on the head or rubbed his back. One sunny day, I noticed a dead bird on the porch outside the front door.

"Where did this come from?" I demanded.

"That stupid cat probably brought him here," my son said, ever the practical one and never wrong—just ask him; he'll tell you. "He chases them all the time."

"But, how could he do that? The bird could fly away."

"Mom. Don't be so naïve," my daughter said. "Cats do that all the time. He just brought you a present."

"Presents like this I could do without. Get it out of here and bury it." I shuddered and went inside After the seventh day in a row of finding a dead bird outside my door and LeRoy standing by with a satisfied look on his face, I had to admit that he had changed his tactics. Leroy was bringing me presents.

Before long we noticed that the bird population was dwindling in the back yard, along with the squirrels and rabbits. My animal habitat was no longer a safe haven for the wildlife we had enjoyed watching. But, LeRoy was still there.

After completing some remodeling on my house, I arranged living quarters for myself and my three children on the second and third floors. We removed most of the household furniture from the first floor, replacing it with student desks and reading materials. A sign on the front of the house announced that THE WADSWORTH READING CENTER was now in operation. Gradually twenty-five or thirty elementary aged children, in groups of three or four, spent two of their after school hours each week with me, brushing up on their reading and math skills.

At first, LeRoy tried to stay out of their way, but his curiosity became more than he could handle, so he gradually got closer and closer to the children. Once he felt comfortable, he ignored them and ruled the house as before. He often came into the reading area, made sure he had my attention, meowed and nodded his head toward the stairway then moved in that direction.

"What's he doing?" Joey asked.

"What do you think he's doing?"

"Looked like he was talking to you," a puzzled Joey mumbled.

"Well, I guess you're right," I agreed. "He was telling me he was hungry. Don't you tell your mom when you get hungry?"

"Yeah," Joey grinned. "But my cat doesn't."

Jimmy and Tony started laughing. "A talking cat," they said in unison high-fiving each other.

From then on, LeRoy was known as the "Talking Cat."

The downstairs living room was sparsely furnished, containing only a sofa, coffee table, chair and a piano. The yellow-gold sofa had a slightly ribbed surface that dipped in two places creating the effect of a three-cushioned seating area. After my children were in bed at night, I often sat on the sofa to read. LeRoy liked to sit on the sofa too, but was not allowed there. True to his determined personality, he didn't give up easily. As he was growing older, he became more set in his ways, knowing what he wanted and going for it.

One night, sometime after midnight, my eyes were drooping as I read when I heard a noise in the hallway that ran between the front and back doors. LeRoy, standing several feet away from me, started meowing and nodding his head toward the back door. He moved a few feet closer to the back door and repeated his motions. When I told him to go upstairs, he ignored me and continued his actions.

Finally, I gave up and got up to let him outside. He kept glancing at me, and moving closer to the door as I came toward him. When I was a sufficient distance away from the sofa, Leroy suddenly did an about face and headed for the sofa where I had been sitting. He dug his claws into the material on the sofa and refused to move. He hung on even when I tried to pull him away. Eventually, I gave up, picked up my books and started upstairs.

"Looks like you win this time, LeRoy," I said and could almost swear I saw him smile.

It wasn't long after this last incident that LeRoy left the house and never came back. We never found out what happened to him but were sure he was no longer alive. If he had been alive, he surely would have returned. Even I had to admit that I missed him, too.

A CHINESE CAT IN A FRENCH BOOKSTORE
By Gabrielle

On September 11, 2002, an unusual browser arrived at Madam Hilda's English language bookstore, Tea and Tattered Pages, on the rue Mayet, a short street at the edge of the St. Germaine district on the Left Bank of Paris.

This browser, a large—make that huge—walking fluff of orange hair, introduced himself as, Ming Lung. He explained to a curious Madam Hilda that in Chinese his illustrious name means Courageous Dragon.

"He has proven himself to be just that," Madam reports.

Ming Lung easily slipped from browser to occupant.

"He has become indispensable to me," Madam says. "He comes and goes through the front window and guards the shop at night when I return to my apartment."

Born in Columbia of German parents, Madam came to live in Paris by a circuitous route. She learned English in the Frence Lycee, and became a doctor of Romance languages in the United States, where she subsequently taught humanities in college.

"But, France?" I ask.

"Many people say they would love to retire to Paris," she says. "I did it!"

So did Ming Lung. It remains a mystery just how he got to Paris from China, but that's what it means to be Chinese, isn't it? Mysterious.

He is obviously of the aristocracy. "He may have royal blood," Madam says. "He hasn't told me."

"Royals are always reluctant to brag," I say.

Madam and I watch as the handsome cat walks to the door, rears up on his back legs and begins to fiddle with the latch. This time, he gives up and jumps effortlessly up on top of the bins of second-hand books resting on the window shelf.

"Sometimes, he gets it open," Madam says, nodding toward the door latch.

This is my third visit to Paris and each time I come to the bookstore. Of course, I enjoy my talks with Madam. Sometimes we sit in the tiny tea room at the back, sipping tea and exchanging stories; but, even if that were not so, I would still come back to see Ming Lung.

"He has many fans," Madam says. "I am under no illusion that they come to see me. It is my Curious Dragon who is the attraction."

Next time you're in Paris stop in and say, "Hello." You'll find Ming Lung downstairs napping among the mystery books or nodding off squeezed on top of a shelf of books near where Madam is perched on her high stool behind the cash register or in his favorite spot on top of the bins in the window where he can indulge his curiosity about the array of people walking by his shop.

We couldn't resist putting in our own cat stories

Turn the page and read three more!

STRAWBERRY
by Gisela Engelhardt Riedinger

Hi, I'd like to introduce myself. My name is Strawberry and I am the most unique cat, let me go back to the beginning and you'll see why.

My first home was in a suburb of Atlanta. It was a nice place...quiet, not too much traffic. You would say, "Why does Strawberry worry about traffic?" Well, you know I do like to investigate and that means crossing the street, so that neighborhood was great. My street was lined with nice homes and there were plenty of trees. Already, I dreamed of climbing those trees.

And then there were hiding places. Hiding places in flower boxes and underneath steps, but most of all the people were all very friendly. So that was the area for my first home.

A lady from that neighborhood, had adopted me and another kitten. I was the Strawberry Blond. The other kitten was an ordinary black color. As you can see, I was the unique one to start with.

That lady had the idea for the two of us to be outside cats. Well, I did not like that much, but I had a lot of discovering to do, so I was a rather busy cat. Climbing the trees was as good as I thought it would be, and the little lizards were great for chasing.

Things were not so bad until I met the lady's dog. Boy what an ugly one, with a face that made your blood curl. Naturally, Blackie and I invaded his territory, so he would chase us. I hid in the bushes or in the flower bed or under the steps, but that dog somehow would find me and chase me out.

Well now, it dawned on me why we were outside cats. Old ugly was inside. So I had to start thinking and find a better hiding place. I thought about the house across the street. It was nice and had a nice lady living there. I just had to get to know her somehow. I noticed she went out to get the paper every morning. Well, I would be ready to slip inside when she opened the door.

Well, I tried and I did slip inside. The lady did not chase me so I was safe. I looked around. Oh boy, a nice soft chair, a sofa! Wow! I was happy. It was time for my nap. The back of the sofa looked soft and there was a basket that if I curled up tight, I could fit inside. It was in a good spot. I could overlook a big area of what the lady called "the family room."

The lady's name was Joanne. She spoke to me softly and petted me and didn't chase me back outside, but she did not feed me. I did not understand, but it looked like I had to go back across the street to eat my dinner which was waiting in a bowl on the porch.

I had just gotten used to comfort and now I had to go back outside. So it went for awhile. I'd go into Joanne's in the morning, sleep on the back of her sofa or in the basket and then have to leave at supper time.

Then the woman who had adopted me had to go on a trip, so she asked Joanne to feed me and look after me while she was away.

This was my lucky day. Now I had my home, I lived inside. Sometimes, I went out climbing trees or chasing lizards or taking a nap in the sun. I also used to like to take a nap on the diving board out over the pool in Joanne's backyard, but the best thing was: No bulldog.

Then I became a mother to two kittens. I didn't know I was going to be a mother, but one night after my adopted mother came back and I had to spend the nights outside again, I felt funny. I hopped up on the window sill of Joanne's bedroom and scratched on the screen. She got up and let me in and then she went back to bed. I curled up behind a small cabinet in her spare bedroom, but I couldn't sleep. What was happening? Soon, when my kittens were born, I found out.

Well, I was too young and skinny to be a mother. Those kittens did not make it, even though Joanne tried and tried to save them for me.

Now, Joanne and my adopted mother decided it would be best if I lived with Joanne, since I had made it clear that it was what I wanted.

Everything was great until another dog came into my life. Her name was Lucky. Joanne brought her home. I don't know why. Why did she need a dog when she had me?

I had to show Lucky that I was here first. She was an old dog and did not fight me, so there was a truce. But I ruled. Eventually, Lucky left for Doggie Heaven, so I had the kingdom to myself again.

Joanne was planning to move; she had retired. Well, I was not sure what that meant. All I knew was it was going to be a change for me and I was not too happy. I thought I could change her mind. So I was super attentive to her and brought her little presents that I caught—a mouse, a lizard. Strangely, she seemed not to like my presents. She thanked me, but she always put them back outside.

Well, the big day came and I was very nervous. I was

put into a box. I was not happy to say the least. We went for a long ride and I don't like to ride in a car. Needless to say, I got sick. Joanne took me to a doctor at the destination and whatever he gave me made me sleepy.

When I was back to normal, I found myself in our new home. Now I had to explore. I checked out every corner of the house and I will say, I liked it. I liked the soft chairs and then there was the sunny Florida room. It faced a pond. I loved lying on the chaise lounge and daydreaming. Then Joanne had a screened area just for me. It even had grass and little bushes. I loved it. I would sit there at night and look at the moon or I watched animals going by. Yes, the new house was okay, but I did miss the pool.

Joanne planned a big trip. Well, I did not like it too much, but I saw the suitcases and that meant a change was coming. Joanne introduced me to a lady who would care for me. I had mixed feelings but I knew Joanne had friends and they were my friends too. I knew they would watch out for me.

After Joanne left, that lady was not too great. She just plopped my food in a dish and she never bothered to talk to me. But everybody else checked up on me so I was okay. That's when I met Gigi, she was one of Joanne's friends who came to see me during that time.

One time, Gigi stopped at the house at night, when the one who was supposed to be taking care of me had gone out. I was outside in my screened area and when I heard Gigi calling me, I thought it would be fun to play hide-and-seek, so I jumped behind a little bush and stayed very still and very quiet. I could hear Gigi calling and calling. Once she even came to the door. I was sure she would see me then and the game would be over, but she didn't. A little "giggle" meow escaped me and she said, "Strawberry! I've been looking all over for you. You scared the life out of me. I thought you were lost."

Silly Gigi, what was wrong with her? I knew where I was. I was right there all the time.

I was happy when Joanne finally came home. Now a new chapter in her life started. A gentleman named Glen entered her life. I liked him at once. I felt he was the right person.

It's funny, but friends and neighbors were concerned about me. I don't know why. Glen and I hit it off. The big day came and Glen and Joanne tied the knot. Now he would be around all the time. I thought things were perfect then, but another change came my way.

Glen and Joanne found another house they liked, so again moving was on the agenda. I was nervous when the man came to load the truck with furniture and I had to wait in the bathroom. Then, finally, Gigi arrived and in the box I had to go, and up and away to the new house.

It was a short trip. I did not see much. After things were organized and I could roam around the new house, I had a good time exploring and I must say I like it here. Lots of room, a big porch where I can sit and dream and watch the dogs go. In fact, I love it here. It is the perfect place.

One of my favorite spots is Joanne's chair. It affords me a clear view of the television set. I sit, paws crossed sphinx-like—after all I am royalty—and watch my shows. I am particularly fond of Jerome Robbins' musicals, especially his ballets. They move me. As a royal cat, I have aristocratic tastes.

I have Joanne and Glen trained to know when I want to eat, or when I want to go out and sit on the glider, or when I want to be brushed, or when I just want to be left alone.

I did tell you that I'm a unique cat, didn't I?

STRAWBERRY GOES TO THE DENTIST
by Joan West

Our resident tabby, Strawberry, had to go to the dentist—well, okay, to the vet—to have some teeth extracted. "Some" turned out to be six. How many do cats have, the standard thirty-two?

For quite some time, she had been demanding in her requests to be brushed, but for her, brushing was different than the usual brushing. For one thing, she liked a stiff brush, not the soft downy ones made especially for cats. For another, she wanted me to hold the brush still while she rubbed first one jaw and then the other against it.

You'd think I would have caught on. I just thought she had itchy jaws until she visited the veterinarian for her yearly check-up. The nice lady vet told us she had "some" teeth that needed to come out.

"She'll feel better," the doctor said. "Well," she amended, "she feels all right now, but she'll feel better with them out."

It was the "Well, she feels all right now" that caught my attention. Who has cat's teeth pulled? If anyone had told my mother she had to have our cat's teeth pulled, she would have contacted the men in the little white coats.

CATS

My mother was not a cat person to begin with. She was not a dog person, either. Let's just say that my mother was not at her best with animals.

When I was six, I had brother and sister cats, Peter and Peggy named after the children in my first grade reader. How my mother allowed that, I don't know. Probably *her* mother, my grandmother Mimi, pulled a fast one and dumped them on her. Mimi was good at playing end runs around my mother, much to my delight.

What I do know is that my fastidious mother was not about to have a litter box in the house. She set about training the cats to use the people facilities; and she was successful with Peter. He didn't read the newspaper while in there, but he did what was required of him.

Unfortunately, she was not as successful with Peggy; however, she did train her to jump onto a designated window-sill and meow when she needed to go out. My mother unhooked the screen, Peggy jumped out, did her duty and jumped back onto the window-sill to be let back into my mother's litter-box-free house.

I digress, but a litter box also plays an important part of the story of Strawberry's teeth. She had begun *not* to use her litter box. I don't think I need go into any detail, except to say that I had begun to wonder why I had allowed her to choose to live with me in the first place.

At the vet's office, I'd told the technician about it, but she didn't have any advice. In hindsight, it wouldn't have hurt to have asked the vet herself, but who's perfect?

A few days later—sometimes I'm a slow learner—I began to put the proverbial two and two together. It was an "aha!" moment—unusual potty behavior and jaw scratching plus a toothache or several of them.

We made an appointment for Monday morning at eight-thirty.

"No food past midnight and pick up her water dish first thing in the morning."

Not even a toothache ever interfered with Strawberry's appetite. We had an unhappy cat on our hands.

I drove, while my husband Glen held her, whispering sweet nothings into her ear in an attempt to keep her from going ape in the car, as is her usual behavior.

When we arrived, another cat and her person were there ahead of us. The woman told the receptionist that her cat was quite stressed and she was worried about the outcome.

In fact, the woman was more stressed than the cat, who calmly accepted the transfer to a sympathetic technician, while her person left in tears.

Strawberry appeared to be uninterested in the entire procedure until shortly before we left when she suddenly threw off enough orange hair to stuff a small pillow.

The receptionist at the vet's office called us to pick her up at two-thirty. She would be a little groggy, the woman said, but most of the anesthesia would have worn off by then.

The anesthesia was still working slightly and the ride was relatively quiet—relatively—and Strawberry actually looked out the window a bit.

Our instructions were: "She may have some soft food tonight, but don't be surprised if she doesn't eat anything. Let her have a sip of water and if she keeps it down, you can leave her bowl on the floor."

Oh? Put down on the floor, Strawberry immediately stumbled over to her place mat where she expected to find food. She took a sip and then a long drink of water and made it clear that something more substantial was in order.

Bottom line: She ate an entire can of whitefish and tuna. Keeping it down was not a problem.

Strawberry sans six teeth was back to normal.

BED AND BREAKFAST CAT AND ZAK
by Glen West

"What was that noise? Was it in the kitchen? Hello, I'm Jericho, the bed and breakfast cat." I open one eye, as is my usual custom, to survey the situation. Nothing amiss. It is my responsibility to guard the most important room in the establishment; the kitchen, of course, harboring all those good things to eat. Already my mouth is watering just thinking about them. "Wait! There's that clatter again!" I open my other eye. "Maybe, I'm missing something! No, I'm right!" I'm scurrying to my kitchen. "Meow! Intruders!"

"Hey, where did that darn cat come from? He'll wake the household! Grab him! Throw him into the meat locker!" the male intruder exclaims.

Before I know what is happening and can jump aside, I'm grabbed by the female accomplice, "Meow."

"Ow! That darn cat scratched me!" she screams, and rightly so, for I am digging my claws as deep as I can into her arm in which she is crushing me. But before I can extricate myself from this dangerous situation, she hurls me far back to the rear of the meat locker. At once, even before I hit the rear wall, I am literally flying through the air, racing for the door. "Bang!" Too late! It slams shut! I immediately jump as high as I can to reach the door lever. "Clink" goes the latch. I'm trapped inside the meat locker! I can't escape. I'll freeze to death! "Grrr!" I'm shivering! Already icicles are forming on my ears and eyelids!

"Zak! Zak." Can he hear me through the massive door? "Zak, Zak, I'm locked in the freezer!"

"What was that?" I'm Zak, the snoot-nosed hound, guardian of that most important front entrance to this bed and breakfast establishment. Nobody, but nobody gets by me! "Growl" I open one eye, a habit I acquired from that darn milk-sucking kitchen guardian cat, Jericho.

"What's going on in there? What's he up to now? It's not even dawn!" I lift myself slowly, ears as long as my snoot-nose, slapping the carpet. Big yawn! I can hear a faint meow coming from the kitchen. "What more trouble is that cursed Jericho into this time? Well let me see! Hey, his milk and water dishes are knocked over! What a mess! He's in real trouble this time! Wait! All the kitchen drawers are open! Look, there are raw meat scars leading to the outside door! There's been a real calamity here! Jericho! Jericho! Where are you? Troublesome cat."

"Zak! Zak! I'm right here. Locked in the meat locker! I'm freezing in here!" I shake more icicles from my back and tail, "Get me out of here, Zak!"

"What are you doing in there, Jericho? Didn't our masters serve you enough fish to suit your fancy?"

"You scrawny kitchen mongrel! Get me out of here before we wake all the guests!"

"Just lift the inside lever."

"I can't reach it, Zak! Help me."

"What happened here? How did you get locked in there in the first place, Jericho?"

"The robbers locked me in here, Zak!"

"The robbers?" I questioned. "Robbers!" I bellow, as I jump as high as I can to reach the outside latch to release my stranded freezing friend. "I can't lift the latch with my teeth or paws! We need help!"

I start barking a mean streak as I hear Jericho's loud screeching meows through the dense heavy door.

103

CATS

The chaotic uproar awakens the housemasters. "What's going on downstairs? Zak is barking like thunder and Jericho's meows are shrieking. Are those two fighting again at this hour? It's not even dawn!"

"You better go down and see." The housemistress replies. "I've never heard them so vociferous. They're frightened about something. Be careful!"

Upon reaching the kitchen, the master asks, "Zak, what's happened here? This place is a mess." Looking around, he adds, "and where is Jericho?"

Jumping frantically against the locker door, I bark, "Jericho's locked in the freezer!"

"All right, Zak, let me reach the lever." As he unlatches the door, Jericho bursts out, shivering, coat covered with frost.

"Oh! You poor little kitty, all wet and cold; here, let me warm you," cries the housemistress, having arrived just in time.

She picks me up, fondles and strokes my poor shivering, almost frozen body. "Purr, purr," I sob, smirking at Zak.

"How do you like that? I saved his scrawny, milk-sucking, mangy, frostbitten, good-for-nothing alley cat and he gets all the attention. I'm out of here!" Head high, tail up, I march haughtily to my bed, sulking.

"Zak! Good boy! Well done! You're a hero," exclaims the housemaster.

I turn at once, tail wagging smartly, eyes beaming, barking repeatedly. "Yes, you're right. I, Zak am a hero! I agree," as he stoops to me nose-to-nose, eyes-to-eyes, shaking my paws.

"Meow! I, Jericho agree profoundly. We are partner guardians of this bed and breakfast."

"Woof! I, Zak consent intensely," getting in the last word.

Story originally published in *A Book of Short Stories* Fireside Publications 2007

THANK YOU FOR READING OUR CAT STORIES

We hope you have enjoyed them!

We would love to hear your comments:
joanpwest@comcast.net
Joan West, Editor

When I observed he was a fine cat, saying, 'Why yes, Sir, but I have had cats whom I liked better than this;' and then as if perceiving Hodge to be out of countenance, adding, 'but he is a very fine cat, a very fine cat indeed.'

James Boswell *Life of Samuel Johnson (1791) 1783*

The end of the Tales !

CATS

CATS

CATS

CATS

Printed in Great Britain
by Amazon

79219784R00068